CAREER ADVANTAGES

AN INTERDISCIPLINARY APPROACH

WALTER K. DAVIS, DBA, MBA

Copyright © 2020 by Walter K. Davis

All rights reserved.

Published in the United States by Walter K. Davis, DBA (DISC Enterprise)

No portion of this book may be reproduced, scanned, sold, or distributed in any printed or electronic form without the express written permisission of the author.

ISBN: 978-0-578-68707-0

Library of Congress Cataloging-in-Publication Data is available upon request.

Printed in the United States of America

To my children, Audrey, Donte' and Brittany. Their patience, maturity, understanding, and inspiration influenced the motivation to transfer my graduate work into entrepreneurial possibilities.

Contents

Introduction 1

1. CAREER ADVANTAGES 4

Career Development: A Personal Fit 6

Discovering Your Interdisciplinary Skillset (DISC) 16

2. EDUCATION INNOVATION 33

Know Your Professional Competencies 36

Graduate Study Impact 38

3. COMPETITIVE ADVANTAGES 45

The Leadership Challenge 47

Career Interdependency 53

STEM Careers 62

4. CONCLUSION: MARKET YOUR SKILLS 85

Publishing Graduate Research Work 87

Entrepreneurship 90

Acknowledgment 99

About The Author 100

References 102

INTRODUCTION

Frederick Douglass's master reacted after finding out how well his "nigger" slave was reading by saying, "learning spoils the best nigger in the world." His master stated that "If he learns to read the Bible, it will forever unfit him to be a slave." The master went on to say, "He would at once become unmanageable, and of no value to his master." Frederick Douglass then realized how he would gain his freedom from slavery. In times during my career advancement, I have personally experienced and understood the depth in mind and spirit that this passage has on certain people in our society. As devastating as it sounds, this context has always given me more tenacity that I needed to accomplish a goal in my life.

Career development is personal, educational, and organizational. It is a fact of two or more things in comparison, having a contrasting effect or juxtaposition. Developing your career happens through a continuous process of doing the following items: understanding yourself, educating yourself, and managing or planning your actions based on current or past events. Professionalism, in combination with higher learning towards career development, is an iterative process that keeps us focused and evolving for succession. Developing a career through skills and knowledge assessment also means building on your past and current career experiences. On the one hand, people hardly ever plan and practice career development.

On the other hand, education is a topic that seems always to be a significant element for career solutions in our society. In reality, no one wakes up one morning and thinks that their career needs to develop. As young people, we follow the habits and behaviors of our parents and those who have the most direct influence on our growth daily. There is a real possibility that education of some form or another may not be a viable option. One way to approach a novel strategy for career development is to encompass an interdisciplinary method of thinking about it critically.

Jamie L. Gallo published work in 2017 exploring interdisciplinary careers and found that one way to grow intellectually and strategically disrupt business through professionalism is by applying interdisciplinarity. Bringing together knowledge from various discipline areas to create one activity is a practical activity we perform every day. For example, in a college setting, we learn the principles of conducting research. This activity might synthesize knowledge from courses such as biology, mathematics, and chemistry to resolve a life sciences problem. To think broadly of a single coherent event in terms of experience coming from various fields of study, people can improve learning abilities, skills, and practical competencies.

As people develop and get older, we tend to move through our lives reactively and not proactively, facilitating our own needs as we see fit without considering the impact of the economic consequences. The importance of applying career development to our livelihood never becomes aforethought. For example, when we encounter some sudden level of cultural or economic change such as family tragedy, employment layoff, or military discharge facilitating our own basic needs, only then do we surmise the possibility of career development as a solution. If we had only planned and predicted the change, we could have applied mitigation through planning and being strategic about the outcomes, whether positive or negative.

Just as staffing talent and qualification priority are essential to an organizations' business success, the same philosophy of acquiring skills, knowledge, and competency level should apply to the career success of people who spend the majority of their lives assessing and preparing for that opportunity. Organizations expend enormous effort and resources, building their staff through recruiting, learning and employee engagement, development, and retention activities. Applying resources and attempt to gain qualified candidates' education and training investment does not seem to keep its value in economic downturns. Socioeconomic influences sometimes do not always guarantee gainful employment opportunities. The effort and expense that a person invests in his or her career must matter in a way that meets the strategic intent of that person's occupational goals in the long run. You are the entrepreneur of your personal career development and management. This venture is your business.

1
CAREER ADVANTAGES

My work in this book endeavor originated from years of experience in business and industry, practical evidence, and my graduate research. More broadly, I used the results of my study in combination with the context of my own industry experience. The attributes of my combined experiences include cultivating my academic education with my professional skill and practice, transforming these into competencies for the benefit of success in various career occupations. The unique novel aspect of my observations and decisions writing about managing my career development came from thinking about the lenses of innovation, business strategy, and the theories of knowledge and critical thinking.

Constructivism theorizes how people learn and absorb knowledge. This theory suggests that people create their understanding and knowledge of the world through experiences and reflection on those experiences. The idea of constructivism goes on to suggest that when students encounter something new, the integration of these ideas must align with previous schemes and skills by connecting the new knowledge to something already known. Students are studying course work completely new and different. Sometimes this concept will result in the student rejecting the ideas entirely. This theory assumes that we are active creators' knowledge requiring students to ask questions, explore, and assess what is known or learned. Students engaging in interdisciplinarity are, therefore, creating their understanding and knowledge of the world through their study choices.

Just as staffing talent and qualification priority are essential to an organizations' business success, the same philosophy of acquiring skills, knowledge, and competency level should apply to the career success of people who spend most of their lives assessing and preparing for that opportunity. Organizations expend enormous effort and resources, building their staff through recruiting, learning and employee engagement, development, and retention activities. Socioeconomic influences sometimes do not always guarantee gainful employment opportunities.

You are the entrepreneur of your career management and development within a community where practicing your intellectual and professional craft is your business. Organizations and multinational corporations depend on their employees to use the principles of each of these subject areas daily to gain competitive advantages. People thinking critically about how to navigate their career goals can adapt these same principles to guide their best judgments and gain benefits.

Let us start by examining the definitions and the literature on three qualitative subjects, innovation, knowledge, and strategy, and how we can adopt these concepts to our model. As a professional evolving with industry experiences and attending college, I learned about terms like innovation, idea generation, knowledge management, and strategy. After I learned what these terms meant, I thought about it, and I realized that we as people had been practicing the components of these ideas long before I knew that corporations and academic institutions took credit for planting them into our society. As I think about the concept, innovation is a process that concerns the improvement of something tangible or intangible.

Career Development: A Personal Fit

Personality and character help to influence positive career advantages. These traits can have positive and negative impacts when planning and making decisions about career goals. For example, public speaking is an important skill to have and can be beneficial in the right circumstances. Some people will react to these decisions differently than others, which can be the difference in how you move forward in your career. Career advantages come with the right opportunity for those who possess these behaviors when others would be at a disadvantage.

When I was much younger, the place where I grew up was always in the news for being one of the worst places to live and be successful. I grew up in a small town in Michigan, not all that far from the city of Detroit. I wanted to become a Neurosurgeon just to help my mother better manage the symptoms of her Epilepsy disorder. I and my younger brother and sister were all she had when things got tough late in the evenings when she could not sleep because of severe seizures. As a disabled single mother raising four of us kids, she had plenty of battles with financial and socio-economic issues.

Over the next ten to twenty years, awareness of self-discipline helped me to understand how I could help other people. Sometimes, making self-assessments throughout your life can be advantageous for choosing the right career path. I later realized that to reflect on what I cared about in my youth, impacted by the obstacles of my environment, the decisions for career choices came quickly for me. To my reading audience, be conscious of your mental capacity to learn and gain more knowledge about certain skills and competencies.

Looking back on my childhood, I did not fully understand how my social circumstances could impact my ability to learn and develop. Continuous investigation of the roles and responsibilities for a certain job position will help you understand how to gain the necessary knowledge for that position. For example, knowing how to perform technical and analytical tasks will allow you to advance and differentiate you from others screened for the same position. These competencies are dependent on one another, and they are also reliant on an individual's vocational behavior. Interdependency is the process of uniquely linking these skills to tactfully develop, improve, and expand your occupational position concerning your career. In various military careers, being physically skilled and not limited to difficult, strenuous activities also has its unique advantages.

At one point, I had to set some new goals for myself and make a career transition that could have been risky in terms of my economic standing at the time. After graduating from a technical college with a Bachelor's degree in Electronics Engineering Technology and working to secure meaningful and established employment, I realized again I had to set a new goal to achieve a better way to more economic freedom. I had a plan, and I intended to carry it out, not thinking of the physical risk or failing to pass any military physical exam. Entering the military would allow me to gain more in-depth technical knowledge that would support and supplement the technical engineering education I had previously acquired.

Soon I realized that I had helped myself identify an important development milestone in my efforts to direct my career and achieve my long-term goal. I was considered "old" at twenty-six when I entered military service. In just a few months completing my basic training requirements, I found myself thirty pounds lighter, stronger, and running faster and farther than I ever could before joining the military. Even though I entered the military at such a late age, mentally, I was strong enough to handle the physical activities and perform well enough to pass every physical test.

My own ability to physically handle activities in all-weather and chaotic wartime environments while I served in the U.S. Army was significant to performing tasks that others could not complete the mission at hand. These hands-on experiences, along with the interactions with other people, gave me more awareness of my ability to learn about how I perform to complete technical and social tasks. Regardless of the coming economic landscape of the late '90s and early 2000s, the fact that I knew how to systematically broaden and improve my newly attained skills from technical school to the military again gave me the feeling committed for the long haul.

The results of my own life experiences and doctoral research concerning the process of how leadership in industry and organizations consider their intellectual capital and make decisions toward competitiveness is the basis of the book. My work and experiences led me to create a workable, practical model called the DISC model, developing interdisciplinary strategies for career advantages. The DISC model is a process that cultivates professional working experiences and academic training to improve certain skills and competencies for the benefit of success in various career occupations. Organizations and multinational corporations depend on their employees to use the principles of each of these subject areas daily to gain competitive advantages.

People thinking critically about how to navigate their career goals can adapt these same principles to guide their best judgments and gain advantages. What is career development? What is our definition of career success? And what competencies are necessary for us to improve and become successful? Systematically, each chapter steps through thoughtful, innovative solutions of how a person could apply these principles to better understand their transformation of skills to competencies that result in optimal career maturation. Individually, each chapter in the book gives the reader a look at the current thought on career development and how people think about what it means to have a successful career.

The result of having a meaningful career is a factor of the value of an investment that a person will put into each opportunity to excel in it. A meaningful career evolves through building a business, opportunities to attain intellectual property rights for a patent or trademark, advanced educational initiatives, or transition from military duty to civilian life. The chapters collectively focus on a person's view of job satisfaction, level of entrepreneurial awareness, and how one's innovative capability may contribute to the positive economic demands in society.

A Career Driven Process

Here we are again asking ourselves why me. Economists and top viral scientists some years ago predicted viral outbreaks. The Bush and Obama Administrations received much research from their advisory councils concerning this very issue (OSHA, 2009). According to these predictions, some level of economic slowdown or impactful recession was inevitable toward 2020. In our lives every day, other people can and have tried to control some portion of our perspective that jobs and careers are somewhat of a place holder for a paycheck to paycheck lifestyle.

There are many factors to indicate that the job market does have plenty of opportunities that can help us at least mitigate the risks of a slowdown in terms of establishing great careers. Thinking more about the benefit of your capabilities needed by industry puts us in a better place for opportunity rather than concentrating on the name of your position. I would rather focus on asking myself, how do I contribute to filling a gap or opposition that my employer is trying to solve? One of the fundamental principles I understood during my time in business and industry, the U.S. military, and in graduate business school is how to add competitive value to the products or services created in the organizations.

The evidence is in those industries that have pinnacled based on demand. No systematic process or level of economic productivity can survive without these valued benefits. Behind this principle are several factors of knowledge management and strategy that sustain organizational survivability. Having the ability to adapt to various environments and a passion for a belief in something helps keep us resilient during these times.

Some people need to feel like their careers deserve attention and that they matter. In fact, for them, their career is a mirror reflection of the lives they live every day. It is their thinking that one depends on the other. What key elements of our skills and capabilities must we mature to effectively pursue a meaningful career? And how do we evolve these elements? The second part of a career-driven process involves lower level sets of principles, such as how to be analytical and how to communicate your competencies. It also illustrates how to cultivate creativity and how to solve problems. Personally, marketing this value to gain employment sustainability can be attained by self-improving on the following factors.

- Academic training, virtual learning
- Growth industries: research skills and interdisciplinary experiences in related careers
- Accomplishments and community volunteering matters
- Entrepreneurship: Some industries no longer require college degrees but require more trade and technically applied skillsets.
- Be systematic and philosophic by showing growth in your resume profile.
- Continue interviewing: Sharing how you solved problems in your current and past positions allows other organizations to see the value of your skillset.
- Working through conflict requires the ability to verbally and literarily communicate with others through transferable skills.
- Dynamic remote work
- Internet networking, sharing the knowledge you have gained.

Analytical or critical thinking is the qualitative process of applying conceptualization to examine a problem, analyzing the context of the problem, synthesizing, and evaluating the outcomes. This process concludes by developing an informed decision or judgment that leads to a practical solution. In industry, certain circumstances drive the use of critical thinking skills:

- A military combat nurse analyzes the order and treats a field of wounded soldiers.
- A chemist evaluates the materials that best apply to a specific manufacturing process.
- An attorney formulates a strategy to best judge whether there is enough evidence to settle a case.
- A marketing manager analyzes customer feedback forms and converts the data into a customer service training presentation for employees.

Critical thinking involves a careful examination of a problem or information in the form of text or data. This analytical process includes understanding the meaning and rationale of the report examined here:

- Data analysis
- Questioning facts
- Information Interpretation
- Determine variances in the data

Sharing ideas and information in a group setting with colleagues is necessary for effective communication. Focus groups apply critical thinking to solve complicated business problems by:

- Situational Assessment
- Verbal and written communication
- Collaboration
- Offering ideas
- Creating presentations
- Teamwork

Creativity often implies using one's imagination to recognize patterns in the analysis. When applying a level of creativity to problem-solving, critical thinking can lead a person to find a unique solution to a unique problem. These qualitative skills cultivate the creative thinking process:

- Predictive analysis
- Imagination
- Conceptualization
- Inference judgment
- Cognitive Synthesis

Another skill people use to exclude making assumptions when analyzing information is the ability to be objective. This critical thinking process allows a person to evaluate a situation without including some level of bias by:

- Being fair to varied perspectives
- Consider cultural ideas
- Practicing reflection
- Make observations
- Be Inclusive

Problem-solving involves situational analysis, integration, and the assessment of a practical solution. Solving problems include five primary skills outlined in a systematically step by step process:

- Factors Analysis – evaluate the causal factors, isolating the contributing circumstances that caused the unwanted situation. Factors analysis involves active listening, data

gathering, pattern recognition, needs identification, and fact-finding.
- Analysis of Alternatives – investigating alternative solutions. Analysis of Alternatives requires forecasting and strategy implementation, teamwork, collaboration, prioritization of alternatives, and brainstorming.
- Forecasting – make decision analysis by evaluating the most significant options. Forecasting involves logical reasoning, formal discussions on clarification, cost, resources, and test development.
- Plan Implementation – the team must implement decisions about alternatives and plans. This process involves project management, collaboration, standardization, and benchmark development.
- Assessments Effectiveness – systems that help to formulate the quality of the alternatives and any barriers past or future must be in place and confirmed to determine whether the solution to the problem is working.

With these key principles, we can begin to understand how to develop planning toward your career goals. For example, use these principles as a guide to making assessments, objectively measure the importance of your competencies, accept the challenges of defining what your weaknesses are. There is an important direct relationship for profitable corporate interests to have a direct relationship with the assets of human capital. The same kind of relationship exists when it comes to being competitive in career planning that helps to exploit your creative competencies for developing your self-branding.

It is very seldom that after your academic training or military duty that you will have the qualitative tools that speak to using the interdisciplinary skills you attained while studying or during years of military training. The following tips will more broadly help to establish a starting point. Occasionally reflect on the important aspects of your immediate and long-term career goals. Working environments change, personal life experiences happen, revisiting what is important during your career planning allows us to prioritize the constructive risk learned while gaining competitive competencies.

In my experience, prioritization helps to measure the relevance of your competencies objectively. Find a mentor who has already developed professional experiences and practical career strategies. Inspiration and encouragement can come from people who have been through experiences like your own. With your plan in hand, a mentor can help you craft and cultivate ideas that you may have. After years of military service, graduate, and doctoral graduate studies, I participated in a volunteer mentoring capacity to help young graduate students and practicing professionals get better at understanding their goals and objectives.

Use your professional environment or volunteering experiences to find opportunities to learn more about how to develop your skills. The theme of this book is to create for yourself the capability of employing innovative ideas. Also, how to discover how to navigate those learned skills and competencies. Gaining interdisciplinary skills happens when cross-functional activities occur and at a time of career asset development. Learn and understand how to manage your career. Remember that changes in your work environment and your own life experiences. Because of the relationships that you have built and the networking skills that you have gained, managing these changes is imperative. Continuously improving your network of others who you can learn from and setting new goals and objectives will help develop the advantages you want to enhance your career going forward.

Discovering An Interdisciplinary Skillset

In the introduction, we mentioned an important fact cited by researchers from the National Career Development Association (2008) that career development is personal, educational, and organizational. Making small improvements is necessary for growth in career planning. During the process of developing career advantages, making small improvements helps us recognize what practical contributions attributed to our skillset satisfy the problems of society. There are references used in later chapters in this book that help support the evidence that career development involves these small improvements. As we also mentioned earlier in the chapter, that managers in multinational organizations have continuously improved their process of building business structures that ensure economic transactions for the benefit of their growth and prosperity.

I discovered a valuable tool while studying marketing in my college education. Market research is a valuable tool used to collect data and information about what makes organizations competitive in their respective industries. This tool can also be applied to establish education and career innovations as we navigate through our competitive journey. Market research influences a person's career advantages by one, identifying opportunities to serve various groups of customers, recruiters, business and industry, or academic working environments. Verify and understand the unmet needs of customers. The test market defines a customer's competition for career opportunities in the test market.

These markets can include occupational and corporate recruiters, industry human resource professionals, military service recruitment, and academic professionals. These individual groups are looking for qualified candidates to discover new knowledge and move it forward. What specific skills and qualifications might they need and want? Certain attributes describe these group's roles and responsibilities. Information found via town hall meetings, medical center job advertisements, news media articles, government agencies, private recruiting offices, and through website advertising such as LinkedIn and Indeed. A second way is to investigate the needs of the various recruiters or human resource professionals who represent academia and industry.

Begin to segment the various professional and industry groups into categories that exploit the specialty career areas that they have to offer. Conducting one on one interviews with academic mentors, military personnel, and healthcare professionals are all great ways to attain their experiences and knowledge on how they obtained their skills for their career professions. A third technique using market research allows you to examine your competitors. Market research is performed by strategic planning and understanding what skills other candidates are offering. By utilizing a candidate's education and work experiences as a reference, you should be able to assess the way you would structure your skillset.

Consider venturing out and performing onsite interviews with these professionals to gather pertinent information that will help cultivate ideas for identifying your specific skills and competencies. Reading job boards, the roles and responsibilities of a job description such as for a supplier quality engineering specialist, for example, can provide immediate important data. One last method helps to clarify your unique value proposition. Value proposition defines the level of attractiveness of the product or service offering brought by your skills and capabilities. The proposition defines how well you perform these abilities helps to determine the level of satisfaction you give your customers.

Organizations seek value from your skills; your skills also help to define your innovative system of how you to start and sustain your own business. The reader should take time and reflect on how well those who benefit from your performance are being satisfied. Evaluation of data and feedback can be valuable to help you maintain a reference point for skills effectiveness and as a basis for improvement. Discovery of your interdisciplinary skillset (DISC) will illustrate how to adapt the concepts of idea generation, skills planning, identifying opportunities, marketing, and testing your competencies and use them to advance career outcomes.

The Innovation Process

Earlier in the introduction, we looked at what it means to acquire an interdisciplinary strategy toward career exploration. With little understanding, it is hard to distinguish which factors help individuals to consistently improve this process, which we will examine in later chapters. We cited Jamie L. Gallo (2017) that one way to grow and strategically disrupt business through professionalism intellectually is by applying interdisciplinary skills. Having the knowledge and understanding of the cumulative skills attained through academic study and cross-functional working experiences can give you the advantage needed to improve learning in a competitive career environment.

Innovation is a process used by entrepreneurs and organizations to make new products or services better and advance in their competitive positioning. Innovation can also mean a new way of performing an existing or previous task or event for the benefit of the business. The goal during and after this process of improvement is to increase revenue, capital resources, intellectual property, customer engagement, and profits. Bean & Radford (2000) asserted that for coordinated organizations driving technology or industry, opportunities in innovation involve efficient improvement and continuous development in the following capability areas:

- Organizational governance
- Policy Planning
- Employee creativity
- Introduction of product or services
- Process improvement
- Supplier relationships

Remember that the heart of this book is to illustrate how to bring value and entrepreneurial performance to those who currently work in business and industry. The book illustrates the concept of value to those who are transitioning from one career field to another. It shows those who are retiring from one career and wish to continue to contribute positively to their own societal goals. For example, the book should give the person who has completed their obligated military commitment some good career ideas and facts about how to develop their interdisciplinary skills competitively.

To understand the qualitative factors motivated by the various real-world, practical experiences and educational lessons gives the reader a start to realizing how to get started in the DISC process. The creation of this personal skills-based process will provide the roadmap to successful career choices, and from time to time, we will revisit this notion to underscore why we need to think critically about the book's motivational purpose. Understanding the context of three qualitative factors of innovation, strategy, and knowledge management will help to provide you with attributes to personal career survival.

In this section of the chapter, we begin to understand the definition and purpose of each of these. In business and industry, these factors help determine certain financial investment decisions, management strategies, and the kinds of relationships and partnerships that will help to cultivate stakeholder value. Integrating these principles and techniques support creating the roadmap mentioned earlier that apply to your career advantage strategy. In the following paragraphs, we will generally illustrate the constructs of each of these qualitative factors to understand how they relate to our career development planning.

Innovation is the process of making small improvements to an existing product or service or creating a completely different or new disruptive product or service. Innovation comes from the transference of knowledge by people to a new product or process ideas, commercializing these ideas for those who would see them as valuable for their own customary or personal benefit. In research published in 2016, human capital defines transactional business as the ability of each employee to contribute to the organization's resources through its own embedded knowledge and capabilities. In business, human capital is a qualitative asset that comprises intangible functional processes that employees engage in to produce valuable tangible outcomes.

For example, it is the tacit knowledge and skill that employees possess to write and install instructional programs that robots use to perform mechanical tasks. The innate ability that a person must be creative gives us a picture of the level of talent that is intricate to innovation. The research study discovered that synergy exists between an organization's inherent ability to be competitive and its human capital resource. Researchers Yaseen, Dajani, and Hasan posited that for international businesses to be competitive and successful, tacit knowledge positively contributes to its ability to create strategies, develop growth and profitability.

The premise of intellectual competencies manifests the collective value of the organization and the knowledge of its employees. Innovation encompasses this through the talent that supports the process. When developing your career advantages, you will have to prioritize, leverage, and manage the unseen resources. This idea also refers to the intuitive human interaction toward your career goals or objectives. Intuitively, just as it matters in organizational psychology, the basis of successful human capital development is a process that has a direct relationship with being competitive.

In businesses, whether large or small, driving the innovation process means creating new value to satisfy customers and markets. Business concepts of innovation focus more on solving market problems, affecting the efficiencies of the process, and the increase in profit and revenue. As mentioned earlier, developing a successful strategy and improving your career involves an interdependent process. As it applies to the individual contributions from a personal perspective, innovation employs continuously improving the attributes and competencies that enable your career and separate you from your competition.

Management expert Peter Drucker once stated from the perspective of the innovator, the process of entrepreneurship is the ability to prioritize and effectively allocate human capital that drives technology changes and the economy. Professionals who contribute to producing innovations and which organizations obtain their success can prepare ourselves for the same outcome for our personal development of our skills and capabilities. In early 2019, a recent study by O'Reilly & Binns found that industries experiencing the most disruptive innovation changes include healthcare, information technology, finance, retail, media, transportation, and education.

In multinational businesses, process influences the effects of human capital performance by a process, innovation, and customer relationships. To understand how these skills align innovation, strategy, and knowledge management work on your behalf. These conditions could essentially put you at a competitive advantage quicker than your counterparts with the same level of academic training and professional experience. Experienced professionals must be creative at handling technological changes that occur in the marketplace and become intuitive about innovation strategy. A person might wonder and ask themselves how managing the knowledge and skill they acquired from professional experiences and education over time helps to be competitively beneficial.

Personal performance and value ultimately are the goal of implementing the DISC model, which is driven by how we manage and integrate these experiences and education to some successful end. As challenging as it seems on a personal career development level, even managers and employees in large multinational corporations learn how to develop, warehouse, and transfer knowledge. Scholars have determined that managing knowledge attained from prioritizing resources has an economic and strategic relationship. And although knowledge management is a social activity, it bears an economic advantage as it relates to cultivating your career advantages.

Managing Knowledge

Knowledge management leverages the skills and abilities to carry out a task towards your branding and positioning to the satisfaction of the customer you are planning to target. The better your competitive agility, the more your exposure to those who would gladly invest in your product or service offering. When it comes to knowledge management outcomes, research supports the evidence that a good knowledge management practice maximizes strategic performance and can translate to personal career value. Studies show that knowledge management processes have a relatively strong explanatory significance of 51 % when it comes to human capital, 75 % as it pertains to organizational capital, and 52 % regarding relational capital.

In one study by researchers, knowledge management processes easily codified related to industries like finance, information technology, healthcare and engineering, acquisitions, documentation of product requirements, data or information transfer, and application. The data from their research helps support evidence that applying knowledge processes in practice has a significant positive influence on the human and relational capital value, which inherently positively drives the transfer of knowledge. When we as career goal-setters systematically use what we have learned through education or business process to establish a policy or set up governing principles for ourselves, this produces a simpler way for us to gain career clarity. Having clarity helps us establish our set of interdisciplinary skills and competencies.

Leadership in large organizations must see the value in their employees and associate personnel regarding codified processes and systems to measure how successful they have become through asset management. Throughout industry and academia, managing codified knowledge has become a process by which skill, competencies, and capabilities can include influential external factors transferred into intellectual assets. Generally, knowledge involves the transfer and dissemination of facts and skills acquired through experience or education, understanding a specific subject area by applied theory or personal practice. According to scholars, knowledge involves human interface and information based on intuition, judgment, and insight into human interaction.

In some industries and academic environments such as managing projects in healthcare systems, these methods and techniques allow professional team members to codify (clear or explicit communication) best practices, organizational memory, past patient documentation, and charts. In a study of aerospace and high technology defense companies, interviews with senior executive officers, directors, engineers, and consultants demonstrated that knowledge creation and transfer structure was related to the organization's competitive advantages. This knowledge is known as tacit or implicit. Tacit knowledge is difficult to transfer from one person to another. This communication becomes explicit after the effective transfer from one person to another.

Writing words to describe the thought or verbally communicating the thought is the preferred method for effective transferability. In most industries that use high technology to process their innovations, complex product or services development occurs in short, concise, and systematic development cycles. The leaders in various healthcare systems understand that innovative thinking helps facilitate or even create new and improved standardized systems among employees and management. We, as individuals, can adopt these principles of codifying experiences and education, thus understanding how to grow and manage our knowledge assets.

Managing Strategy

The context of the book regarding the process of implementing the DISC methodology illustrates corporate leadership structures and their strategies around the decisions of creating value from its intellectual capital. Leaders in industry and academia understand that product or services development cycles mean contrasting the interdependencies that these processes are based significantly contributes to overall competitive advantage. Industrial entities invest large portions of their revenues for their leadership in understanding operational and financial strengths, weaknesses, opportunities, and threats. When executive management has effectively taken responsibility for its resources, the benefit can directly influence the overall value creation process for the company.

In my experiences in business and industry strategy formulation in real-world practical applications such as engineering and medical technologies drive the idea of conceptual knowledge management frameworks. I spent many years working in business and industry, experiencing how corporate management integrated strategies between departments and divisions to process their products, whether it was medical devices or aerospace subsystems. As I studied and researched further the effects and influences of strategy and knowledge management of products and services developed in large organizations, I discovered other perspectives on the issue. Within the strategy process, organizations expend many resources sustaining this knowledge framework.

This process often involves market positioning, supply chains, intellectual property management, and operational functionality, such as, for example, quality initiatives to sustain competitive advantage. My research focused on the challenges of how to manage technology transfer, solving problems for entrepreneurs, and how industry solves complex technical problems for consumer applications. This systematic emphasis on strategy and decision making invokes integration of actions over time towards value positioning. In other words, these actions give these professionals the ability to effectively manage how skills and competencies towards achieving ambitious goals and objectives equal strategic management leading to asset growth. Using the principles of strategic management, ordinary people can prioritize their skills and capabilities to adapt and facilitate improving career outcomes.

Academic research has been performed by professionals who help provide social-based data on the subject. Let us look at a few of the literary references that helped me gain many facts about how to integrate these ideas into the model of discovering interdisciplinary skills that contribute to career advantages. Some researchers investigated strategy by compartmentalizing it as a way that executives in organizations plan their business processes and strategize their market outcomes. Strategic management is the process of planning and prioritizing investments made on the organization's critical value drivers of its intellectual capital assets.

The first step is to determine which drivers enhance these knowledge assets. The next step is to determine which of the organization's total assets contribute to the largest portion of its competitive advantage. Professionals in business and industry who spend their careers developing products or valuable services and operating businesses must understand how to acknowledge what variables constitute their skills-based interdependencies. As we have defined earlier in the chapter, these interdependencies help prioritize the organizational intellectual capital that determines industry value.

Remember that interdependency is the process of uniquely linking these skills to tactfully develop, improve, and expand your vocational position regarding your career. Qualitative analysis or the behavioral assessment of the value drivers (whether knowledge or relational) emphasized important prioritization principles to accomplish competitive advantages. Other researchers' outcomes examined the context of strategy and structure regarding the interaction of the lower level managerial activities, the design of strategy, managing product development activities that occur in organizations toward competitive advantages. Managers in large and small organizations plan their strategies based on the goals of the organization and increasing awareness required for specific activities.

There are examples of this interdependency process in complex manufacturing industries. In 2013, various researchers published findings that bolstered this perspective. Those entrepreneurs and innovators in business and industry decide what interdependencies or relationships exist between protecting product innovations through competition and the process by which to codify and catalog those innovations. These technical and business analyst professionals recognized there were awareness problems regarding the practices of effectively managing intellectual capital assets. In my own experiences, investment opportunities for product protections in new product development would decrease in the absence of technological advances, improvements, or future innovations.

Perez-Cano and Villan-Altamirano examined interdependencies of processes, systems, and management practices regarding the types of decisions that justify the reason to gain intellectual property rights. Their research demonstrated how interdependencies work to influence complex product development decisions. People develop innovation dependence during the creation of their ideas. These motivations can often lack interdependence. The magnitude of the relationship between an organization's level of effort, type of innovation, and codification is dependent on strategic choices. The combination of utilizing strategy and management increases the chances that managers can effectively influence change within their organizations.

Managers representing product or services development must consider the capabilities of marketing, engineering, the technical level of employees before making critical intellectual property rights decisions. Those professionals who are innovators within their industries implement decision framework approaches for purposes of understanding the specific interdependencies in organizations. The relevance that process and product interdependencies have on their outcomes depend on several relationships. These relationships occur between their degree of codification and their intellectual assets. Remember that communication becomes explicit after someone who makes a statement about an issue effectively communicates this to another person receiving the message.

As discussed earlier in the book, we, as individuals, must learn the principles of codifying experiences and education and learn to grow and manage our knowledge assets. Specifically, an industry that had stronger relationships in their internal human resources knowledge were more apt to use property rights protections as a competitive advantage. Usually, as investments in research and new product development in organizations increase, the goal is to achieve a level of knowledge that improves on its development processes while driving profitability. In my experiences in business and industry, product and service development, professionals must coordinate their knowledge and strategic management abilities.

Successful development depends on the dissemination and exploitation of innovation to protect knowledge assets from imitation by their competitors. Successful development in the electronics and aerospace industry suggests that strategy defines an innovator's ability in a complex new product development environment to identify, learn, understand, and communicate. Studies in competitiveness showed that there is still a lack of the needed organizational communication through the work experiences and the perspectives of more efficient ways to value creation and knowledge management. More knowledge of the different innovation activities helps managers and employees to determine the strategies used to protect from competitor imitation.

Integrated product team members who find difficulties in identifying better ways to learn and manage a knowledge culture, lose the benefits of being innovative, and the threat of imitation is greater over time. Demartini and Paoloni's methodology illustrated strategic management principles that integrate action research to discover the practices of innovators through their knowledge and expertise, environmental and cultural experiences. As many industries adapt to the dynamics of the new technological environment, managing their resource efficiency, profit improvement will only begin to address the importance of the strategy behind value creation. Added value largely depends on the products and services created by those employees and managers and according to economic principles as intangible assets in the overall business portfolio.

Later in 2015, Survilaite, in collaboration with other strategy management scholars, asserted that the critical factor for competitiveness predicts the strategic management of knowledge and information. Professionals working on completing projects in complex technology industries need the competence and capability of creating effective process-oriented communications to be successful. Again, adopting the principles of understanding how your unique skills and abilities to your career help to uncover the importance of your competencies, accept the challenges of defining what your strengths and weaknesses are. As we illustrated earlier in the chapter, there is an important direct relationship in creating vocational space for being strategic about career planning that improves your self-branding. Just as in business law, managing knowledge is complicated.

Businesses operate to find the value of their knowledge assets while systematic planning for a long-term process to increase their revenue with many barriers. It is critical for academics and business professionals to understand that during the innovation process, good outcomes depend on concise communication of efficient knowledge management processes that correlate to effective product development. Large and small business projects comprise the interdisciplinary functions needed to identify new product markets, understand the prioritization of customer needs, and prioritize task coordination. The interdependencies that negatively affect knowledge assets in business include things such as new development costs, lack of product information, and the lack of market resources to handle competitors.

In organizations, capitalizing on these interdependencies by investing in intellectual capital improves strategy. This strategy ensures the business perspective of allowing a more effective approach to increased shareholder value. Innovators who understand the interdependencies between the components of intellectual capital and its development environment improved the value creation process. Over time synchronicity is established by the change to sustain innovation competitiveness effectively. Other sources of information that provided support to the ideas that strategy and management in this chapter came from themes that evolved from the analysis of the strategic planning documents, policy and leadership improvement, skills, and competencies in colleges and universities. University technology centers' strategic plans reveal four comprehensive interdependent factors for each of the categories.

Goal one describes the transference of legal knowledge and clinical experience; goal two describes the initiative to establish core competencies; goal three focuses on the specifics of lawyer planning, investigation, and client empowerment. For example, under these goals, the strategic plan suggested that the academic rigor of its law and engineering programs align with the proposed knowledge management category. Research sponsored initiatives performed by staff would align with the strategic goals and objectives under the knowledge management category. University technology centers train prospective attorneys and scientists to be responsible, effective members of society, committed under the program to up to 700 hours of clinical hands-on legal tasks, and 40 hours of working with community stakeholders under real-world projects.

University technology centers expand their revenue base to facilitate a working relationship between faculty and staff to provide intellectual property protections developed out of ongoing research projects. In business and industry, these factors help determine certain financial investment decisions, management strategies, and the kinds of relationships and partnerships that will help to cultivate stakeholder value. Creating products or services that benefit society involves activities that depend on other development activities. Ultimately, the effective integration and implementation of these practices for new product development help to create effective competitive strategies. Integrating these principles and techniques as we emphasized in earlier lessons helps drive our ability to focus on strategies that make career advantage effective.

2

EDUCATION INNOVATION

The success of any organization, whether large multinational or small entrepreneur depends on developing human knowledge and putting that knowledge into practice to improve the business. An organization can be a young group of graduate electrical engineering students, a promising team of nurses discovering enormous patient care innovations, a military platoon creating eyes on strategic processes. Education innovation means to continue to find unique ways to learn to stay relevant. In any organization's collective knowledge is protected by its confidentiality policies. According to policies and management trust in strategic partnerships, knowledge is developed over time by the loyalty and intellectual abilities of its employees. These abilities drive the subject matter practices, and improvements give the organization a competitive advantage.

The business information cultivated by the employee's skills and expertise developed over time is also known as intellectual property or trade secrets. These valuable secrets and intellectual property are assets transferred through the process of creating and contributing this knowledge. Not often do organizations work hard to cultivate this complex information and how these assets are vital by their employees. Some tangible examples of this intellectual property that you, the employee, can become aware of and how the value of your knowledge has contributed to the firm's overall success:

- Innovation by scientific and engineering discoveries, product or service designs
- Initiatives or publications developed, planned or proposed that helped sell products or services
- The methods of practice, internal policies, techniques, and processes are taken to create products or services
- Company slogans, logos, special product names or markings
- Customer non-disclosures and agreements
- Strategies developed for business endeavors and marketing planning
- Technologies in the form of systems and software

According to a joint research initiative by the University of London, Department of Management Birkbeck, UK, 476,000 new businesses are started every month in the United States. Wow! I wonder who and with what types of resources are starting these businesses? Well, I believe I can explain with a little education, skill, and experience. It is critically important to understand that what we learn, no matter the source, can make a life-changing difference. These differences simply mean that you can immediately get the benefit of creating new knowledge and being prosperous from it relative to our career objectives.

Let us look at statistics, for example. In my experience, this area of mathematics is the least liked and the least understood by millions of college undergraduate and graduate-level students. Ratios and proportions are simple statistics that may be the most widely used statistic in mathematics that we use in our everyday living without even realizing it. A rate is a quantifiable relationship between two values, equal or not equal, that gives the number of times one of the benefits contains within the other. A proportion is simply a statement that two ratios are equivalent.

Statistics is one subject that is the most practically used but little realized in daily life and many academic and social disciplines. However, for students, it is the one subject most challenging to comprehend that they should even take the course to solve fundamental research problems. Statistics involves a researcher who systematically collects, organizes, performs analysis, interpretation, and reports data based on the design and limitation of an experimental model. Decision-makers determine the viability of predictions based on data and information. The data or information does not always provide clarity to the context of the message and its assessment.

The intent is the systematic organization of the numbers represented by data. This organization methodology provides a tool for describing the variability of it, giving a clearer picture of the interpretation of the desired message. In basic research, there are several principle concepts and processes to grasp to understand why this tool of mathematics is so useful.

- An experiment starts with an assessment of the effects on a phenomenon to discover new knowledge about that phenomenon.
- Proposed methods to perform the assessment or study are approved.
- Experiment by collecting data.
- Apply a statistical analysis methodology to evaluate the differences and inferences in the data that was collected.
- The researcher reports the interpretation of the findings and argues the factors and evidence considering the experiment's design and parametric limitations.

It is usually best if the reported information can be generalized as much as possible to the general population. Generalizing the info is just one example of a skill that is often far too underestimated by our society and institutional culture. Around the globe in business and technology, expertise and transferable capabilities are still expected to produce sustainable outcomes that can keep us motivated towards career success. A global company operates as a unique corporate culture in facilities around the world yet provides products or services in a single location.

A multinational company builds its products and services in self-contained manufacturing facilities across the globe and operates these facilities with local human resource structures. Nike Corporation, for example, produces a product creation center in Italy that focuses on the talents of marketing and merchandising. In the Netherlands, Nike has soccer apparel and product distribution support centers that use design, finance, legal, and online sales talent to keep that market's expectation running. In Japan, Nike has multilingual engineering specialists that support manufacturing and operations to help produce its designs.

Know Your Professional Competencies

In another example, learning outcomes of higher education institutions such as colleges and universities should be the impact on our men and woman of the U.S. Armed Forces experientially. These academic tools help to develop and integrate innovative approaches to business problems they will encounter. These are one example of the professional competencies that start to impact critical thinking processes.

Globally and in diverse environments, statistics is a powerful tool that helps us gain the following skills and experiences:

- Communicate strategic approaches and apply them to business practice and planning.
- Apply critical thinking to complex business problems and develop innovative opportunities.
- Communicate descriptive and inferential data using analytical techniques to support evidence-based decision making.
- Develop ethical concepts and integrate these into sustainable business models.
- Allow expert cross-functional professionalism in any business or technology discipline area.
- Develop collaborative leadership techniques applicable to relationships, partnerships, and alliances.

From automotive manufacturing to a surgical emergency room operation, this technique applied to optimize any work activity. Process capability is a tool that allows those developing and building a product or service to do the work with fewer steps, more time, and safer while at the same time improving the quality of those products. The lesson here is that we can motivate the next generation of bright scholars and inventors. Learning is cumulative, and it serves as the building block for subsequent cognitive development. We should continue to teach our young people the value and importance of education and what it means to be innovative and entrepreneurial. Again, the DISC model illustrates that through adaptation of new complex skills, the career professional gets the benefit of interdisciplinary learning.

Graduate Study Impact

In one of my doctoral-level statistics courses, while studying Business Strategy, I learned about Markov's decision analysis techniques used to optimize a business problem. These same techniques apply to compare debt to equity in the annual reports of just about every major multinational company on the planet! In another example, STEM (Scientific, Technology, Engineering, and Mathematics) students have a firsthand opportunity to understand a complicated statistical technique called process capability. In manufacturing operations, this technique simply involves process optimization, which allows employees to make better products while improving the quality of those products.

The lesson here is that we can motivate the next generation of bright scholars and inventors because learning is cumulative, and it serves as the building blocks for subsequent cognitive development. We should continue to teach our young people the value and importance of education and what it means to be innovative and entrepreneurial. By the time you make it through your residencies, the individual specialty courses, the research methodology, reading the most pertinent research, posting your writings for discussions, the postings, and the discussions of the doctorate program weariness seems to set in. Getting back that energy it took to fulfill the doctorate work after you decided that this would be a good thing to pursue is key to thinking about what the work was worth.

The excitement and career focus that seemed to exist at the beginning now called for a replenishment. The question presented here is not to suggest that the MBA degree program has less value or academic expectation than the DBA degree program. The differences in the MBA and the DBA is more broadly expanding the idea of knowledge expertise to developing or creating new knowledge.

Beyond the tenant of a management problem solver as in the MBA program, as a DBA learner, this new knowledge environment offers a deeper understanding of the mechanics of the business or scientific processes and the tools for empirical analysis. For example, the research model that you create could explain how customers perceive the product or service created by your organization and how their response will open new market opportunities.

The same model could also be used in a contextual form to train or orient graduate and undergraduate professionals to better seek out their future career direction. These skills and capabilities have broad applicability to your career competency and possibly other organizational case studies as well. My DBA core coursework covered the advanced study, project work, and applied research contributing new knowledge to business theory and, more importantly, my professional practice. I advanced my studies by leveraging my past professional experiences as an engineering specialist with a broad focus on business strategy and data informatics, technology transfer, and process capability in business. My research dissertation work examined the effects of strategy and knowledge management on decisions to protect innovation.

In general, the Master's in Business Administration (MBA) program focuses on the practicality of general business management and leadership style in organizations. The practical approaches to leadership and business development accompany other applied managerial coursework. My MBA core coursework covered the business and technological aspects of accounting, applied statistics, business communication, business ethics, risk management, managerial economics, entrepreneurship, marketing, and operations management. My project thesis work focused on the effects that optimization and process capability have on product quality in new product development environments.

Personal awareness and reorganization of an action plan to think about the many career options that are now necessary for learners to reflect on. Taking on the DBA degree program did not just offer to learn how to read academic journals and disseminate the statistical significance of the informatics that lie within the research. I completed the DBA program aligning my technology and business experience illustrated in my dissertation by developing a model that explains the conditions of how legal and product professionals share knowledge assets. The model also provided critical elements of planning decisions to implement protections of their intellectual property during new product/services development.

Whether your career focus is healthcare, marketing, human resources, or engineering, the point is that the DBA program comprises more significant critical career elements comprised in than you expected to understand that positively impacted your current and future career goals. Your current professional work as an MBA practitioner compliments a scholarly transformative skillset that not many other people have expertise. The DBA provides this skillset. In contrast, the program prepares the learner for more impactful knowledge generation with practical case examples as subject matter evidence of the theoretical coursework.

As mentioned previously, the details of earning a DBA degree, two main outcomes contribute to the commitment of the 4-year term. The program contributes to the learner's business and analytical research knowledge, and it also attributes a more defined development of the practical understanding in the learners' everyday professional discipline. The learner eventually uses these skills, which become applicable to their specific professional discipline. The DBA learner must endure several internal moderations of the dissertation before taking at least two external examinations. The dissertation learner will have their work revised numerous times before the final approval process by the doctoral dissertation committee.

Also known as a terminal degree, the holder of a Ph.D. requires the learner to develop original work leading to a dissertation and defense. After 4 to 7 years of study, creating and publishing research, the Ph.D. offers a quicker path to academic tenure as a full teaching faculty professor in a university or college setting. In general, the Doctor of Philosophy (Ph.D.) program focuses on developing fundamental academic knowledge. As with the DBA degree, the Doctor of Philosophy Ph.D. is the highest academic educational qualification in business, healthcare, or information technology that can now be obtained in the U.S and abroad. Students prepare for research readiness in the Ph.D. program.

Students also learn how to write and publish articles from their research. These programs share some similarities, research methodology, and creating new knowledge. The Doctor of Business Administration, or otherwise referred to as a DBA, is a terminal research doctorate awarded to graduate-level students based on project-based work, business, or market research and examinations. The learner of both the Ph.D. in Business

Management and the DBA will need to accomplish courses in scientific methodology and management theory courses. Courses in scientific methodology cover statistics, quantitative or qualitative research, experimental design, and survey studies. The fundamental objective of taking these courses is to give the learner the skills to become a competent researcher.

The Ph.D. student's primary goal is to develop research questions based on theoretical knowledge due to the gaps in existing theory to publish in business and academic management journals. The Doctor of Business Administration, or otherwise referred to as a DBA, is a terminal research doctorate awarded to graduate-level students based on project-based work, business, or market research and examinations. The average duration of the degree program set by the European higher education standards of the Bologna Process is typically four years of full-time study at a minimum. Management in the National Science Foundation and the U.S. Department of Education, both based in Washington D.C., recognizes the DBA as a research degree and an equivalent to the Doctor of Philosophy (Ph.D.) program.

There are two primary outcomes that the DBA degree contributes to the learner who is willing to take on the 4-year commitment. The program provides to the learner's business and analytical research knowledge, and it also attributes a more defined development of the practical understanding in the learners' everyday professional discipline. It is to the benefit of the learner and the school of choice that the learner has some level of experience in business, not to mention those who hold executive-level or strategic management roles within the organization. When choosing to take on a DBA degree program, here are some ways to keep your focus on success.

- Have a good reason and a clear vision for why you want to complete the Doctorate. Learn from those who have committed to complete the program. Students should understand the importance and the commitment of what this level of education will mean to your career goals and your life outside of classes.
- Whether its healthcare, market research, information technology, project management, or business management, and no matter where your country of origin is, have a passion for your field of study and understand the implications of its relationship to your level of skill and competencies.
- A doctorate offers pragmatic, practical competencies to your career objectives and increases in your performance outcomes. U.S. job markets and salaries tend to vary, whereas, in other countries, wages tend to be constant across disciplines.
- Residencies give the learner an in-depth environment to further rouse their purpose for discovering disruptive innovations that fit the goals of the dissertation. As a matter of preparation for entry into a Doctoral program, one option to get exposure to the discipline area you might be interested in is taking on practice-based seminars. Just as in Ph.D. programs, workshops can prepare you to have answers to questions that pertain to having an outline for the dissertation process.
- Search at the beginning of the DBA program for a knowledgeable, enthusiastic, savvy dissertation advisor, and committee members. Scholar training is the essence of the hard work ahead, and the DBA program is not to come easy. When you think about it critically, this is the personal challenge and purpose for doing the program.

Expect failures during your time in the program. Immediate results while participating in coursework will not always come as you expect. To learn the lessons of the research, it will sometimes take weeks to realize the results of an experiment or case study writing. It will be your passion in the end that will move you forward to success.

3
COMPETITIVE ADVANTAGES

What does leadership mean in business and industry? Sometimes leadership is a process-driven strategy. The effort of administration within the organization helps to develop new initiatives, utilize resources, and enhance the organization's internal ecosystems. Research would suggest that barriers are institutional. When managers understand that these factors contribute to the overall schedule and scope of the company, from a growth standpoint, the development of strategic capability adds to the organization's adaptability to lead in products and services to successful commercialization.

Researchers of behavioral and management sciences found that strategic management is how the element of leadership in various international corporations achieve and sustain competitive advantage in their respective products and services innovations. Leadership means impressing progress and breakthroughs upon those who believe in something more significant than the current status and economic position. It is their perspective that strategic management is achieved systematically and by a process emphasizing strategic analysis or positioning, the strategic options that guide decision making, and finally, the integration of strategy to action.

With added adaptability, management in firms can improve their capability and strengths. These investments, process innovation, knowledge assets, and product differentiation occur systematically. Global organizations operate throughout the world, teaching their management teams and employees lessons in the business realm to stay ahead of the competition. These teams learn the intricacies of business strategy, critical thinking, and decision making. All it takes is the intellectual effort of these many lessons and a handful of leadership to realize how strategic approaches help to formulate critical decision-making enhancement. Through research at the Wharton Business School involving more than 20,000 executives to date, six skills have been identified that, when mastered and used in concert, allow leaders to think strategically and navigate the unknown effectively: the abilities to anticipate, challenge, interpret, decide, align, and learn.

Strategy expert Robert M. Grant noted that all organizations, no matter the type, have some mission to pursue a purpose. In his words, "strategy is about winning." The methods selected to achieve that purpose comprise the organization's strategy. In 2012, business strategy researchers Thompson, Strickland, and Gamble defined strategy as the competitive moves and business approach that managers are employing to bring in customers, grow the business, and achieve the targeted levels of organizational performance. For industries perfecting this concept, moving forward is the key.

Three critical elements exist here: resources and capabilities, the competitive market, and tools and techniques. These ethical questions focus on competitiveness, managerial decisions, and linkages between what is current and the future. These questions affect the success and survival of business enterprises that one would have to ask for streamline strategies in an enterprise to work. Would it work? Suitability means the overall rationale of the policy. Consider whether the plan would address the critical strategic issues underlined by the organization's strategic position. What tools do leaders provide to their teams to think strategically? Can it be made to work?

Feasibility means having the resources available as part of the strategy regarding developing the product or service. Resources include funding, people, time, and information, or cash flow in the market. Team building occurs with internal critical thinking skills in mind. Will they work it? Acceptability means that the employee expects a certain performance outcome (mainly shareholders, employees, and customers), which can be return, risk, and stakeholder/s reactions. The point that the "people perspective to entrepreneurship" and cultivating competencies are essential factors here.

The Leadership Challenge

Competitive and market goals and financial performance determine the vision or mission statement for the business and set the direction and standard for commercial and demand results. Sustaining competitive advantages means that management must build practical barriers to keep its competitive advantage. Differentiation is the process of developing resources and capabilities. Strategic analysis decisions illustrate how the industry conditions, often on a global scale, influence the creation and execution of strategy and a method of effectively creating a competitive advantage against industry rivals.

A firm can acquire resources and capabilities in two ways: it can buy them, or it can build them. Resources consist of three categories: tangible (finances), intangible (intellectual property), and human (skills and knowledge) linked to organizational structure and management systems. Market forces conspire to deplete profits. Shaping keen insights into the right strategies requires the ability to deal with ambiguity in charged and often stressful circumstances. The latest research finds that a minimal number of companies create the most economic profit.

The research also shows that a significant amount of good companies outperforms even in so-called harmful industries, where the average financial benefit is less than the market average. How do they do it? In other words, where do powerful strategies originate? The company must ensure that it is prepared and willing to act on an approach once it is adopted. Strategic thinkers question the status quo. Only after careful reflection and examination of a problem through many lenses do they take decisive action. Making decisions require patience, courage, an open mind, and where business strategy includes access to markets, customer targeting, product processes, and technical capabilities.

Targeting a specific customer segment is necessary to develop useful products or services that meet specific customer needs and requirements. Requirements affect the decision of the customer to purchase the product or service. These include product offerings and the positioning of those offerings within the competitive environment. Technologies provide the basic capabilities and the associated processes used in developing or delivering them to the marketplace. The business processes and functions include the core capabilities of a firm.

They are the basis of a firm's competitive strengths and weaknesses, which make up the core competencies of the firm. Strategic processes improve these capabilities. Within the firm, the final element of strategy access to its market or customers. Implementing strategy depends on both the functions and business processes that support its strategy. These capabilities consist of product or service creation, functions and procedures, and product or service delivery and satisfaction functions and processes. An organization's features and business process capabilities and skills are central to strategy implementation.

The Importance of Career Development

The creation of patterns, integrating these practices into everyday life, and interacting with external societal changes, constitutes developing your career path. Steps to achieving these attributes involve decision making, integrating trends, mastering competencies, educational attainment, communicate a task-specific skill set, and understanding economic conditions that will provide value over your lifespan. This lifelong process means transitioning towards a better future for yourself and anyone who may be impacted by your succession. It has been my experience that the evolution of developing a career through behavioral integration of the steps presented earlier and the creation of a few other specific factors.

- Using my work experiences as a guide to the next employment opportunity
- Reflecting on the process of attaining my previous employment
- Reflecting on the value I achieved from my previous work experience, what did I learn?
- Did my academic education and vocational training fit the roles and responsibilities of each job?

The process of determining what you're good at in terms of a successful career involves improving not just the fundamental problem solving, communication skills, and competencies that sustain employment but also on the quality of higher-level qualitative attributes that enhance your strategic career goals.

Critical thinking is the qualitative process of applying conceptualization to examine a problem, analyzing the context of the problem, synthesizing, and evaluating the outcomes. For example, the advancement of these attributes may include critical thinking, analytical, and creativity skills that focus on the ability to be involved in teaching in a university setting, entrepreneurship, healthcare consulting, and business startup. To this end, this process concludes by developing an informed decision or judgment that leads to a practical solution. In industry, certain circumstances drive the use of critical thinking skills:

- A combat nurse analyzes the order and treats a field of wounded soldiers.
- A chemist evaluates the materials and decides how they will best apply to a manufacturing process.
- An attorney formulates a strategy to best judge whether there is enough evidence to settle an intellectual property case.
- A marketing manager analyzes customer feedback forms and converts the data into a customer service training presentation for employees.

In her recent literary work, "The Job: Work And Its Future In Time Of Radical Change," award-winning author and veteran journalist Ellen Ruppel Shell takes a hard look at factors affecting the nature of work and jobs in the United States and abroad. Ellen Ruppel Shell examines how the future of work and occupation may be more of a challenge than it is an American dream. The author suggests that Americans spend six times more being busy in our careers than we do spend time with family. She emphasizes in her chapters the fact that work and jobs in these times do not give us the benefit of satisfaction in terms of feeling successful in our careers.

Within certain chapters, she points to uncertainties that evoke the risk that, at any time navigating through our careers could end up in failure. According to the author, the question of whether Americans deserve a purpose-driven life, a liberal education, and more social science-based educational initiatives may provide some level of functional independence.

And that through collaborative initiatives, private industry, and government entities might find improvement in public policy and economic innovations toward sustaining rewarding work in the future. Leaving us with some recommendations toward a better understanding of the possible solutions to the problem, the author stated, "to only focus on skills and training is not enough." The author also stated, "a better approach is to retrain our thinking, find new ways to use technology to leverage the power of people."

Specifically, some level of educational acumen combined with professional experiences assists in improving the productivity of the occupation or job that a person performs. The emphasis in the last chapter unveiled that the effective use of education, advanced skills, and experience, which can result in communicating these attributes to success for entrepreneurial outcomes. Publishing research work, building a business brand, and gaining intellectual property patent and trademark rights are examples of transitioning skills and competencies into improved economic stability and opportunities.

The material in this book intends to answer the question of how to implement an effective knowledge management strategy in career development, implementing these elements systematically and effectively might mitigate negative outcomes to the process of career development. Career development benefits both the individual and their organization.

Occupational Choices

There is always the chance that someone before you performed the same kinds of work, had the same set of skills, and possibly improved on similar capabilities as you. The difference may be, however, that you experienced living your life very uniquely. At the time, it is these unique life experiences that set us apart from one another. According to the research and findings of Donald E. Super, the approach to developing better career outlooks led to understanding three perspectives for the individual. These perspectives have continuity in career interdependence and developing one's career goals through direct life experiences. They also include understanding how pursuing a career involves adapting to the interdependency of multiple social roles and vocational behavior.

Super's theory of occupational choice, coupled with vocational guidance, emphasized how an individual seeking career success could even predict that success. This view formed the fact that the various positions and occupations a person held during their lifetime defined a career. This sequence of occupational choices by the individual also included pre and post vocational activities. After the development of a model, the theory considered a person's career patterns based on the sequence of occupational changes over some time.

In many ways, the idea that Super asserted relates to the idea that the sequence of career outcomes that an individual occupies during her or his working life was interdisciplinary. In the end, people base their career decisions in the interest of what they believe in; this is the view from the perspective of ambition, certain scholastic or technical abilities, and other self-acquired attributes. Personality traits, a person's character, and socio-economic factors help determine the vocational behavior mentioned earlier. In a bit more detail, let us examine factors that will influence career development leading to career interdependence.

Personal character attributes to career development. These attributes, for example, can be in the form of entertainers, musicians, and comedians. Individuals who are skilled and knowledgeable about certain facts. People whose higher learning and technical attributes such as those skilled in science and technology provide a need for society in many ways. Someone who is physically superior in performing various tasks will have an advantage in meeting specific requirements over others without those abilities. These professionals perform athletics and physical feats that can transfer to financial wealth.

Some people have an inherently social and economic benefit, which allows their circumstances to impact their development in a specific career field. These people have the understanding and knowledge of their environments and can provide their social talents to deal more with poverty, underserved communities, and unemployment. Taking the best of their cumulative talents, individuals could create a path for occupational choice and career success under the various jobs and positions they held. This way of critically thinking about career success could help to fuel tools for further competency development.

Career Interdependency

In my experience, skill and competency are natural attributes and abilities gained and developed through academic education or training. Depending on the occupational endeavor, the level of employment of a person, the measure of workforce productivity equates to the accomplishment of vocational training. For a worker to complete the required tasks of his or her employment responsibilities, natural talent relates to educational or vocational acumen. These preferences exist at higher learning institutions. Military occupations, STEM professions in industry, healthcare, and business innovation are a few of the professional specialty areas that this topic will be emphasized more on in the coming chapters.

    The level of academic training is important when considering the type of occupational goal that a person is planning to perform. Grade school and high school education teaches us the knowledge skills and competencies to understand phenomena, process, or economic event and recognize the productivity needs that fulfill an economic construct for these. How much education or vocational training is enough to prepare you for a successful transition? The level of academic or vocational training obtained must accommodate and help drive productivity outcomes in the chosen occupation for the worker in their roles and responsibilities.

    It is my experience, for example, that a U.S Army Soldier whose daily tasks are deciphering coded messages hidden within radio frequency signals needs skills in communication, problem-solving, decision analysis, writing, and reporting. The education that a person needs to perform his or her work responsibilities is contingent on the specific tasks of the job, vocation, or business venture. It is my view that any level of academic education in collaboration with practical and experiential working knowledge increases the chances of career security. Career interdependency evolves from the evolution of career satisfaction, is thought to be comprehensive, and iterative in practice.

Vocational improvement, together with the elements of higher-level education, critical thinking and analytical skills, and professional experience, creates a level of motivation endurance. Developing a successful career strategy is interdisciplinary and interdependent, takes some time to accomplish, and by no means a simple process to implement amongst the challenges of everyday life. In the early 1990s, scholars published findings that suggested synthesis of numerous academic disciplines by students seeking higher learning aligns with interdisciplinarity.

Students sought to interconnect knowledge and skills, to synthesize coursework from science, societal issues, and technology programs. As a result, many social scientists addressed developed new research combining two or more disciplines as an approach to teaching experiential programs related to real-world problems. Examples of interdisciplinary studies include topics such as aerospace engineering and bioinformatics. Others are telemedicine, patent and trademark law, and mechatronics. Although somewhat different in theory and practice, multidisciplinary deals with the parallelism of fields, where teams of professionals from these specific fields progress on projects to create outcomes as a result of the collaboration across various disciplines. These programs encourage the possibilities of career interdependency and student enthusiasm, which fuel the development of transferable skills. Transferrable skills in this context relate to critical thinking, mass communication, intellectual comprehension, and analytical assessment.

Interdisciplinary approaches from the perspective of education allow students of complex academic fields to comprehend the necessary interconnections for the sustainment of cross-disciplinary concepts. Students exposed to this approach gain a deeper understanding of how different discipline areas include interrelated skills to answer some of the unique problems in complex systems. Interdisciplinary approaches from the perspective of professional practice-based experiences then allow students to pursue employment to excel at having the competitive advantages they prepared. Research to create new knowledge dealing with complex problems requires analytical assessment, and the integration of economic, social, and environmental issues. Critics have argued the point that the level of difficulty with learning in these types of programs can have negative effects on one's motivation and intellectual ambition.

As a "next-generation" social scientist, I can acknowledge successes of these programs through my own practical experiences in military service, working as a government analyst, and publishing academic research. Recent university and college STEM (scientific, technical, engineering and mathematics) programs across the U.S. and in other countries have helped to cultivate interdisciplinarity, which has supported the emergence of new public needs and professions. Another way that students can gain the benefit of learning these skills is to apply traditional course room theory to practical laboratory experimentation at a low level. In these current times, technology serves as a disruptive incubator cultivating interdisciplinary skills, thus teaming with business and industry, bringing together some of the challenges of real business problems.

During the time between 2015 and 2019, innovative processes and academic knowledge continue to be created inadvertently by the outcomes of recent products and services through industry research and development. In 2016, noted Indian social scientist and activist Chetan Sinha supported the idea that interdisciplinarity neither considers discussion of thought or study. She posited that the process of interdisciplinarity achieves a systematic interpretive synthesis. The system synthesis is an iterative process and provides the creative integration of knowledge assimilation by studying interdisciplinarity.

Finally, in the real practical world, the approach to gaining interdisciplinary skills starts with either problem solving or asking thought-provoking questions about an issue or policy. The added professional value of cultivating interdisciplinarity by bringing together a comprehensive understanding of separate ideas provides students with the opportunity of attaining reasoned decisions, new knowledge, perspectives, and interpretations. Examples of the idea of achieving interdisciplinary skills and their adaptation to a real practice-based application are evident through business owners and entrepreneurs operating innovative companies and product engineering teams working to develop products or services.

As I noted earlier in the chapter, I applied my experiences in business and industry strategy formulation showed me how the application of skills to practical applications that drive the idea of conceptual knowledge management frameworks. As I studied and researched further the effects and influences of strategy and knowledge management on decisions in large organizations, I noticed the relationship between these concepts and interdisciplinarity. Career professionals also expend practical and educational resources toward vocational success, constantly building their competencies. This process for active professionals also involves market positioning, supply chains, and intellectual property management to sustain competitive advantage amongst other professionals.

These programs encourage the possibilities of career interdependency and student enthusiasm, which fuel the development of transferable skills. Transferrable skills in this context relate to critical thinking, mass communication, intellectual comprehension, and analytical assessment. Using the principles of strategic management, ordinary people can prioritize their skills and capabilities to adapt and facilitate improving career outcomes. Different from interdisciplinarity is the concept of multidisciplinarity or the quality of being multidisciplinary. Here, experts tackle solving problems in parallel with each other to create outcomes as a result of the collaboration across various disciplines.

My case study research, which I include in summary here in the book, involved asking questions about strategies for managing knowledge and competitive advantage in business. The open-ended questions intended to capture how managers and technology professionals manage the technology transfer process to solve complex technical problems for consumers to apply to their livelihood. I asked various professionals to reconstruct important details of their own experiences and help establish a baseline to help identify effective methods of transferring internal knowledge and how this knowledge creates innovation. These professionals managed the knowledge base in their organizations for employees who contributed in some way to producing the products and services that led to corporate growth, whether small business owners, large organizations, and government entities.

The case study examined the advantages that product developers, entrepreneurs, and executive managers have when thinking critically about innovation and the value that knowledge has on competitiveness. Technology transfer involves steps for disseminating and exploiting methods in business to governments to industry and manufacturing, improvements in process capability, materials decomposition, legal litigation, and other technological developments. This process usually occurs from the person who owns the innovation transferring it in one form or another to another person or organization. My point in presenting a summary of my academic research is to highlight how it relates to factors that drive career advantages. These factors strengthen the career development planning of many professionals working in business and industry.

The approach to technology transfer in business and industry is different than it is in colleges and universities. The integration of courses like biology and analytics predicates complex outcomes that real-world problem solvers investigate. Integrating courses such as mechanical engineering and electronics creates interdisciplinarity. In late 2013, Al-Aali and Teece published findings that illustrated how efficient management processes help to expedite processing in filing for patents and trademarks for attorneys who represent large multinational organizations. In other companies that manufacture and process complicated systems such as aircraft, plastics, internetworking telecommunications, biomaterials, and financial risk instruments, seek secrecy and licensing protections.

Their research suggested that having an efficient management process is important to management executives considering intellectual property protection, enforcement, and growth. Product and services innovation includes the skills and competencies of employees and other professionals. They inadvertently have a stake in the outcome that contributes knowledge and experiences toward the success of the introduction of innovation to the marketplace. I interviewed professionals educated and experienced in various legal professional tasks, patent, trademark knowledge, academics, and government regulatory activities involving process improvement and management.

Product development processes require collaboration and the strategic coordination of obtaining tacit or explicit knowledge for the discovery of innovation as determined by teams of professional experts. The questions I asked, like how to share experience in your environment, how are strategies for competitiveness formulated between product development groups, and how is competitive advantage regarded during innovation creation sessions evoked critical thinking and qualitative perspectives. Managing these skills promote decision analysis between the different employees during the innovation process.

Improving these processes includes a strategy from start to finish, the development phase, and whether the decision to protect that knowledge is feasible for future growth. Employees who work in technology-oriented organizations use methods such as benchmarking, business formation, and change management as techniques to measure and compare business processes and performance metrics to industry best practices. Other interdependent factors during question and answer sessions provided evidence that analysis tools such as cloud-based software, performance-based scorecards helped managers monitor operational activities between product-based teams.

Employees in organizations, business owners, entrepreneurs, and research students collaborate to develop new products. They are motivated by the rewards of their work to implement various forms of asset protection for competitive advantages. Other vocational interdependencies from employees factored into the synergy of innovation and making small improvements evolved from decision making and knowledge transfer. These professionals also supported the idea that internal decision-making systems established organizational governance to meet the financial goals and objectives of the organization. More specifically, organizational practices that adapt strategic practices for individuals to plan for career development like the following. Like understanding workforce needs as corporate managers do, individuals can:

- Identify your skills and capabilities through self-auditing. Planning career development by assessing your abilities.
- Always try and understand whether your current professional skillset is still practical and whether there may be a need to reorganize or participate in some retraining.

Make sure that your talents determine whether you remain qualified for specific roles and responsibilities.

- Read the job descriptions posted by the company and find out what skills are required.

- Prioritize your skills from most transferable to most technical.
- Make sure that there is a plan to improve your skills.
- One way to know whether the work offered by an organization aligns with the skills that you possess is always to be aware that actively planning helps keep oneself focused on improvement.
- Create a people network in the community to find someone with the knowledge and competence you need.

Boost your level of satisfaction and motivation in your skillset in the work that you produce.

- Feeling pride in the work an individual performs and the tasks that produce good outcomes are always self-rewarding. Satisfaction in individual productivity tends to create a feeling of motivation toward an entrepreneurial spirit.
- These outcomes eventually let you know that your skills are valuable so much so that possibilities for self-employment or a domino effect on your career success.

STEM Careers

In previous chapters in the book, we continued to emphasize the vital aspect of how organizations expend their resources to build their staff with recruiting, continuous training, employee engagement, and retention. To the job seeker, career development fulfills an adaptation to the economic dynamics of work, types of jobs, and the management of workforce requirements. Economic downturns can dampen a person's attitude toward skills development. As we have mentioned many times before in previous chapters, socioeconomic influences sometimes do not always guarantee gainful employment opportunities. It is my view from lessons in my life that no matter what your culture, creed, gender, heritage, or indigenous background you came from, influential leaders and matriarchs, lessons about moving forward in life meant making small changes.

The one guarantee for every person motivated to advance their career is the fact that small changes in lifting attitudes, increasing motivation, and improving your skills base will benefit the chances of career advantages. After we have answered the questions of what career development is, what is our definition of career success, and finally, what competencies are necessary to improve and become successful thinking systematically helps us develop a plan. Once we discover and understand the interdependencies that uniquely relate to our vocational patterns, we can begin the process of implementing the DISC model.

As we move forward in challenging times, we reiterate the point that the effort and expense that a person invests in his or her career must matter in a way that meets the strategic intent of that person's occupational goals in the long run. You are the entrepreneur of your personal career development and management. It turns out that this plan of action evolves the notion that this venture is your business.

My work developing the DISC process model helped me cultivate my professional working experiences and academic training, improving specific skills and competencies that benefited my navigation through various career occupations. With this experience, I want to continue to move knowledge forward, helping to educate younger students and professionals starting businesses and competing in business and global markets. The intent of the DISC model reflects how the advantages that organizations and multinational corporations depend on assist their ability to gain competitive advantages. Management teams in organizations notice the innovation occurring in the business operations of their competitors.

Factors that remain to be items of contention for employees who have advanced in skill and competency center around compensation, knowledge retention, and on-the-job training. Continuous skills development promotes motivation and satisfaction, and always necessary from the perspective of the employer. Despite the award of bachelor degrees, master's degrees, professional doctorates, or Ph.D. degrees, new perspectives on strategy and innovation justify the need to address the various human resource issues that employees encounter. Not always does an individual know the proficiency of their skill set to perform the roles and responsibilities in demand. Let us also remember these necessary steps:

- Understand the workforce needs.
- Determine your talents and qualifications.
- Develop a plan to improve by moving forward.
- Enhance your STEM proficiency.
- Evolve your entrepreneurial spirit and execute your plan.

This section of the chapter illustrates some of the interdisciplinarity of real-world careers offered to the public every day. Be aware of the jobs and opportunities found during job hunting in all forms of media and equivalent networking platforms. As more enhancement of your skills provides more opportunities, also be aware that most job descriptions never change. One advantage of a skilled job hunter during exploration by verification and validation is to re-evaluate awareness of the occupational choices available in the job market.

Enhancement to your skillset involves adding interdisciplinary competencies. For example, the novice musician is talented with understanding live instruments; however, to blend the right sounds to singers' vocals will need the skill of understanding computerized technology to enhance the final product. This small improvement increases the value of the musicians' vocational talent and market outcome. This slight adjustment in skill improvement at the same time increases the musicians' entrepreneurial opportunities. Again, as we navigate through a global technology-intensive environment, the need to improve individual interdisciplinary skills puts a priority on productivity and workforce requirements.

Another way to enhance the principles of the DISC model is to guide ourselves with small improvements and analysis of the current job market and the competency landscape. We have all witnessed within our underserved communities the frustrations of negating the knowledge of the STEM educational advantages from our youth. We all probably know the depth and the ramifications that this causes, especially to underrepresented minority groups. Career advantages negate the vocational opportunities that education in science, math, economics, and technology has had on underserved communities.

The more reason for recommending the lessons, experiences, history, and promotion of understanding that this text provides to the reader. Traditional STEM fields offer high earnings potential and involve understanding the interrelated competencies of interdisciplinarity. Central to this idea, grounding in science, engineering, technology, and mathematics prepare students, business owners, and entrepreneurs for innovative and emerging opportunities. There are some fields in STEM where specialized certifications complement and add more specific knowledge to traditional academic education and on-the-job experience. Non-traditional STEM fields have evolved to add vocational value and career advantages to the discipline areas such as art and media, music, life sciences, and the physical sciences.

Research has shown that prerequisite preparatory courses allow the student to accomplish a proportionate amount of knowledge, fulfilling the long-term requirements needed for appropriate skills development. The reader should notice in the STEM examples below, the roles and responsibilities, required skills, and education requirements. From the lessons of the context in various chapters in the book, there may be skills not carefully emphasized or examined that should be in these descriptions. For the student, the context highlights the importance of the relationship between interdisciplinarity and the benefit of acquiring STEM skills.

The reader should also understand that the context from previous chapters intends to highlight the strength in these skills. For the professional, business owner, and entrepreneur, the context highlights the importance of the relationship between interdisciplinarity and the benefit of career advantages. A few of the examples of the STEM opportunities I present here have helped people think about their long-term strategies toward career advantages.

Science

Biophysicist/Biochemist

Roles and responsibilities: Biochemists and biophysicists study the physical and chemical principles of living things.

Required Skills/Experience: These scientists manage laboratory teams and monitor the quality of their work, review literature and the findings, prepare technical reports, and present research findings to engineers, and other colleagues. These scientists work to evaluate cell development, growth, heredity, and disease to solve a problem. Some positions in government require U.S. Citizenship and an active DoD Secret clearance to perform this work.

Biochemists and biophysicists use:

Advanced technologies, lasers and fluorescent microscopes, and x-ray computer modeling software for determining three-dimensional structures of proteins and other molecules to conduct scientific experiments and analyses.

Education Requirements: Scientists in this field need a Ph.D. to work in independent research-and-development positions beginning their careers in postdoctoral research positions. Many biochemistry and biophysics Ph.D. holders begin their careers in temporary postdoctoral research positions learning specialties to develop a broader understanding of related areas of research. Most Ph.D. holders have bachelor's degrees in biochemistry, biology, chemistry, physics, computer science, or engineering. High school students prepare by learning courses related to the natural and physical sciences.

Microbiologist/Virologist

Roles and responsibilities: Microbiologists and Virologists work in research and development laboratories conducting primary research or applied research. These professionals study microorganisms such as bacteria, viruses, algae, fungi, and some types of parasites to solve problems.

Microbiologists use:

Computers, sophisticated laboratory instruments, electron microscopes, and advanced computer software to do their experiments.

Required Skills/Experience: These scientists plan and conduct complex research projects, perform laboratory experiments, and supervise the work of biological technicians. These scientists manage laboratory teams and monitor the quality of their work, review literature and the findings, prepare technical reports, and present research findings to engineers, and other colleagues. These scientists work to improve sterilization procedures or to develop new drugs to combat infectious diseases. Some positions in government require U.S. Citizenship and an active DoD Secret clearance to perform this work.

Education Requirements: Scientists in this field need a Ph.D. and have at least a bachelor's degree in microbiology, biochemistry, or cell biology. University coursework includes microbial genetics, microbial physiology, elective classes such as environmental microbiology, and virology. Students also should take courses in physics, statistics, math, and computer science to have a broad understanding of the sciences. Many microbiologists and virologists Ph.D. holders begin their careers in temporary postdoctoral research positions. These students learn specialties to publish research, become university professors, and develop a broader understanding of related areas of study.

Business Administration/Management

Financial Analyst

Roles and responsibilities: Financial analysts assess the performance of stocks, bonds, and recommend collection of investments to guide businesses and individuals making investment decisions.

Financial analysts use:

Computers, advanced computer software, and sophisticated analytical software tools to do their trend analysis and statistical processes.

Required Skills/Experience: These professionals prepare reports, evaluate current and historical financial data, and determine a valuation in companies to assess trends in business. Financial analysts work in banks and government assessing the strength of management teams. Some positions in government require U.S. Citizenship and an active DoD Secret clearance to perform this work.

Education Requirements: Most educational prerequisites to becoming a financial analyst, require a bachelor's degree. After attaining a bachelor's degree in finance, economics, or business management, the work requires a license to sell financial products. These require sponsorship by an employer, four years of qualified work experience, and pass three exams. Business analysts in this field begin their careers learning specialties, including accounting, economics, finance, statistics, and mathematics.

Management Analyst

Roles and responsibilities: Management analysts propose ways to improve efficiencies in small businesses and large multinational organizations. These professionals advise management teams on increasing revenues, profitability, expenditures, and reducing costs. Management analysts conduct organizational studies, develop management systems and assist executive management in operating more efficiently and effectively.

Management analysts use:

Computers, advanced computer software, and sophisticated analytical software tools to do their trend analysis and statistical processes.

Required Skills/Experience: Analysts organize information to be improved, conduct onsite observations and interviews, recommends new systems and organizational changes to develop solutions or alternative practices. Management analysts often specialize in healthcare or telecommunications, and government. Certified Management Consultant (CMC) designation can complement graduate or undergraduate education and experience and may give jobseekers a competitive advantage. Some positions in government require U.S. Citizenship and an active DoD Secret clearance to perform this work.

Education Requirements: Most educational prerequisites to becoming a management analyst, require a bachelor's degree. Students obtain a bachelor's degree in business, management, economics, accounting, finance, marketing, psychology, and computer and information science. A bachelor's degree provides the entry-level requirement, followed by a master's degree in business administration (MBA).

Medicine

Emergency Medical Technician/Paramedic

Roles and responsibilities: Emergency medical technicians (EMTs) and paramedics respond to emergency calls, assess the condition of a human patient, performing medical services, and transporting patients by water rescue, ground transport, and by helicopter or aircrew services to care for traumatic injuries.

Emergency medical technicians use:

Biomedical computers, computerized maintenance management systems, cardio-pulmonary medical equipment, surgical devices, automated external defibrillators, and advanced search and rescue equipment to perform paramedic and survival operations.

Required Skills/Experience: Emergency medical technicians perform cardiopulmonary resuscitation (CPR), bandaging wounds, and life support care. These professionals report their observations and treatment to physicians, nurses, or other healthcare facility staff. Other specific duties include medical equipment inventory and maintenance of equipment. Emergency medical technicians also have backgrounds in military service, usually from active service in the United States Coast Guard, U.S. Army, and U.S. Marines.

Education Requirements: After completing high school education, emergency medical technicians typically obtain a Bachelor of Science in emergency medical technology offered in medical technology programs. High school students prepare by learning courses related to the natural and physical sciences.

EMTs can enhance their experience by studying a course in biology, chemistry, physics, computer science, or engineering. Certifications complement traditional education, such as the cardiopulmonary resuscitation (CPR) certification at the state level.

Surgical Nurse/Informatics Nurse Specialist

Roles and responsibilities: Registered nurses work with physicians and other medical specialists in healthcare teams. These medical professionals work in various healthcare environments and oversee the work of licensed practical nurses, nursing assistants, and home health aides. Registered nurses' duties and responsibilities have varied tasks and activities; for example, a surgical nurse works alongside Neurosurgeon physicians aiding in brain surgeries in hospital operating rooms.

Registered Nurses use:

Biomedical computers, computerized maintenance management systems, cardio-pulmonary medical equipment, surgical devices, automated external defibrillators, and advanced search and rescue equipment to perform paramedic and survival operations.

Required Skills/Experience: These professionals consult and collaborate with doctors and information technology specialists, maintain the information security of patients' records, evolving information technology and databases, and lecture on proposed laws about innovative health information systems. Registered nurses also have backgrounds in military service, usually from active service in the United States Coast Guard, U.S. Army, U.S. Air Force, and U.S. Marine. Some positions in government require U.S. Citizenship and an active DoD Secret clearance to perform this work.

Education Requirements: Registered nurses have at least a bachelor's degree in nursing, or a diploma from an approved nursing program. Registered nurses must be licensed. Programs in Nursing include courses in anatomy, genetics, biology, physiology, microbiology, behavioral sciences, and liberal arts. These programs can be completed over a period of four to five years. Clinicians must earn a master's degree, with some performing research obtaining a doctoral degree.

Pharmacologist

Roles and responsibilities: Pharmacologists research medications and test new drugs to see how the human body interact and reacts to these medications. These medical scientists also test medications by studying tissue and cell samples. The research determines the appropriate dosages, side effects, benefits, and safety measures.

Pharmacologists use:

Computers, sophisticated laboratory instruments, electron microscopes, and advanced computer software to do their experiments.

Required Skills/Experience: Research and testing, experimentation of drugs and medications, and evaluating pharmacological studies. A pharmacologist performs research to test new medicines to treat rare diseases. Some positions in government require U.S. Citizenship and an active DoD Secret clearance to perform this work.

Education Requirements: To become a pharmacologist, students begin their undergraduate studies in life sciences or a related field. A bachelor's degree in life sciences involves biology, chemistry, microbiology, physiology, and genetics and includes courses in chemistry, math, biology, and physics. Research, writing, and communications courses complement the sciences curriculum to learn how to write grants and publications. Additional educational training is needed to perform as a practicing pharmacologist. Pharmacologists need either a Ph.D. in pharmacology, a Doctor of Medicine, or a Doctor of Pharmacy. Further research and laboratory training requires Postdoctoral pharmacology training to gain additional knowledge and experience.

Military/Trade

Crime Scene Investigator (CSI)

Roles and responsibilities: Professionals working as crime scene investigators perform criminal investigations at military installations, coordinate with other federal law enforcement agencies, war crimes, and antiterrorism. The U.S. military employs criminal investigation divisions (CID). The U.S. Army, Marine, Air Force, and Coast guard assign crime scene special agents, for example, at times with the Navy Criminal Investigative Service (NCIS).

Crime Scene Investigator use:

Computers, advanced computer software, and sophisticated analytical software tools to do trend analysis and create statistical processes.

Required Skills/Experience: Crime scene investigators collect evidence, perform experiments, conduct interviews, and process crime scenes. These professionals often collaborate with medical experts, physical and life scientists, information technology specialists, and participate in legal municipalities and courts, writing summaries and reports. Agents may assist in federal activities where counterterrorism efforts, war crimes, and with leaders in military operations. Some positions in government require U.S. Citizenship and an active DoD Secret clearance to perform this work.

Education Requirements: Becoming a CID agent can expect a combination of college and training. Colleges and universities have recently offered degree programs where students can specifically apply to CID career opportunities. College and university programs offer criminal justice and forensics science courses at the bachelor's and master's levels. U.S. military schools provide specialized training, such as the Military Police School at Fort Leonard Wood, Missouri.

Information Technology Specialist/Officer

Roles and responsibilities: Tasks performed by an information technology specialist involves analysis and problem solving of digital networks, troubleshoot local area networks, wide area networks, and Internet systems. These specialists provide support routine maintenance of their organization's networks and advise computer users through phone, email, or in-person visits. Information technology specialist collaborates with other engineering professionals, computer systems administrators, directors, and governments that support wide complex infrastructure.

Required Skills/Experience: Performs testing and evaluation, ensuring correct network operation and regular maintenance to Internet systems. Information technology specialists also have backgrounds in military services, enlisted and officer levels, usually from all branches to include the U. S. Coast Guard, U.S. Army, U. S. Air Force, and the U.S. Marines. Some positions in government require U.S. Citizenship and an active DoD Secret clearance to perform this work.

Education Requirements: To become an information technology specialist, students begin their undergraduate studies in computer science, engineering, and technology. A bachelor's degree and master's degree in computer science or electrical/electronics engineering includes courses in math, statistics, advanced mathematics, programming, microcomputers, software engineering, electronics theory, and physics. Research, writing, and communications courses complement the sciences curriculum to learn how to write reports and summaries.

Some certifications obtained by the professional complement undergraduate programs include Cisco Certified Network Associate (CCNA), Cisco Certified routing and switching systems (CCNP), and Cisco Certified Network Technician (CCNT) certifications. Senior IT professionals pursuing system management or administrative career positions obtain either a professional doctorate in information technology or computer science or a Ph.D. in information technology. U.S. military schools provide specialized training, and an online college and university programs.

Engineering/Computer Science

Product Engineer, Radar Engineer, and Analyst

Roles and responsibilities: Product engineers working as Radar engineers develop Radar models, communications interface, system simulations, and perform sensor analysis against missile and hypersonic ground and aircraft electromagnetic threats. Tasks include making system/component performance assessments, performing verification and validation of dynamic electromagnetic acquisitions, track, and discrimination of radar algorithms. Radar engineers analyze, assess, and characterize the performance of system data processing components. These professionals use data analysis techniques to evaluate system performance impacts, perform root cause analysis of observed behaviors, collaborate with other product development engineers and scientists.

Radar Engineers use:

Computers, advanced computer software, and simulation tools to do modeling could develop scripts and analytical tools in MATLAB, Python, Java, etc., and create statistical processes.

Required Skills/Experience: Radar engineers work on product teams, developing new products and system capabilities, developing subsystem specifications to meet customer requirements, planning, coordinating, and supporting large scale manufacturing activities. Other tasks include field engineering, writing reports, performing market analysis, and presenting at conferences.

These professionals often have experience in various engineering or science discipline areas like software engineering, computer science, or mechanical engineering. Radar Engineers and specialists also have backgrounds in military services as officers and technicians, usually these branches of the military; the U.S. Coast Guard, U.S. Army, U.S. Air Force, and the U.S. Marines. Some positions in government require U.S. Citizenship and an active DoD Secret clearance to perform this work.

Education Requirements: To become an information technology specialist, students begin their undergraduate studies in computer science, engineering, and technology. A bachelor's degree and master's degree in computer science or electrical/electronics engineering and technology includes courses in math, statistics, advanced mathematics, programming, microcomputers, software engineering, electronics theory, and physics. Research, writing, and communications courses complement the sciences curriculum to learn how to write reports and summaries.

Senior-level professionals pursuing system management or administrative career positions obtain either a Ph.D. or a professional doctorate in business, management, computer science, engineering, or technology or information technology. U.S. military schools provide specialized training in radio frequency engineering and computer science, and online college and university programs.

Chemical Engineer

Roles and responsibilities: Chemical engineers research to develop new and improved manufacturing processes. Engineers monitor chemical process performance and, by using controlled methods, establish procedures to separate the components of liquids and gases and those that generate electrical currents. Chemical engineers help plan, layout, and build production equipment and evaluate their processes to ensure compliance with safety and environmental regulations. Other development tasks include estimating production costs for management assessment, performing field engineering, writing reports, performing market analysis, and presenting at conferences.

Chemical Engineers use:

Computers, advanced computer software, and simulation tools to do modeling could develop scripts and analytical tools in 3D structural modeling, MATLAB, Python, Java, etc., and create statistical processes.

Required Skills/Experience: Chemical engineers' direct chemical and material operations and apply the principles of chemistry, biology, physics, and math to these operations to solve problems. Chemical engineers help plan, layout, and develop production equipment and evaluate their processes to ensure compliance with safety and environmental regulations. Other development tasks include estimating production costs for management assessment, performing field engineering, writing reports, performing market analysis, and presenting at conferences.

Education Requirements: Chemical engineers attain a bachelor's degree in chemical engineering or a related field. To become a chemical engineer, students begin their undergraduate studies in computer science, chemical engineering, trigonometry, calculus, and materials science. A bachelor's degree and master's degree in chemical and materials engineering includes courses in math, statistics, advanced mathematics, chemistry, physics, biology, materials science, computer and software technology.

Research, writing, and communications courses complement the sciences curriculum to learn how to write reports and summaries. Senior-level professionals pursuing operations management or administrative career positions obtain either a Ph.D. or professional doctorate in business, management, chemical engineering, or materials science. U.S. military schools provide specialized training in chemical sciences, and an online college and university programs.

Social Science

Linguist

Roles and responsibilities: Linguists convert and relay information from one spoken language to information comprehended by another person in another spoken language. These professionals compile language information, are proficient in two or more languages, apply cultural knowledge for translation, and speak, read, and write fluently in at least two languages.

Required Skills/Experience: Linguists convert messages from spoken communication, working in various environments often for large multinational corporations, the governments of other countries, and the military defense services and embassies of other countries. These professionals often collaborate with medical experts, in business, physical and life scientists, information technology specialists, and participate in legal municipalities and courts, writing summaries and reports.

Education Requirements: A bachelor's degree is typically needed to become a linguist with requirements from coursework in social sciences, computer technology, and a focus on studies in languages such as Arabic, Chinese and African dialects. Research, writing, and communications courses complement the language and other science curricula to learn how to write, translate, and report policy-related summaries. Senior-level professionals pursuing management or administrative career positions obtain either a Ph.D. or a professional doctorate in business, management, and linguistics. Linguists also have backgrounds in military services as officers and technicians, usually from all branches, including the U.S. Coast Guard, U.S. Army, U.S. Air Force, and the U.S. Marines. Some positions in government require U.S. Citizenship and an active DoD Secret clearance to perform this work.

Telemedical Counselor/Psychologist

Roles and responsibilities: Under normal circumstances, Psychologists investigate and research the cognitive, emotional, and social behaviors of the interactions between people. Through observations and interpretation, the results of their investigations lead them to make improvements to behaviors by supporting patients with counseling. New processes and procedures include using technology to close gaps in the knowledge of the field. Over a distance, Telemedical and telebehavioral counselors use video conferencing to deliver health care services into the patients' home, workplace, and to the community.

Required Skills/Experience: Psychologists and telemedical professionals conduct scientific studies behavior and brain function, test and diagnose patterns of mental disorder. Other important tasks include identifying organizational issues, interviewing patients, conducting experiments, recommending specialized medicines and treatments to understand better and predict behavior. Researchers in this field write articles, publish research papers, and share their findings and results to the academic and industrial communities.

These professionals often have experience in various psychology, clinical counseling, education, and human services discipline areas. Telemedical professionals and specialists also have backgrounds in military services as officers and technicians, usually including the U.S. Army, U.S. Air Force, and the U.S. Marines. Some positions in government require

U.S. Citizenship and an active DoD Secret clearance to perform this work.

Education Requirements: To become a pharmacologist, students begin their undergraduate studies in life sciences, statistics, and experimental procedures or a related field such as education. A bachelor's degree in life sciences involves biology, physiology or psychology or education, and human services. Additional educational training is needed to perform as a practicing clinical counselor. Psychologists and telemedical professionals need either a Ph.D. in psychology, a Doctor of Medicine, or an advanced degree in education specialist degrees (Ed.S.) or human services and either certification or licensure to work.

Further research and laboratory training requires Postdoctoral psychology training to gain additional knowledge and experience. Research, writing, and communications courses complement the sciences curriculum to learn how to write grants and publications. Professionals in this field also have backgrounds in military services as officers and technicians, usually the U.S. Coast Guard, U.S. Army, U.S. Air Force, and the U.S. Marines. Some positions in government require U.S. Citizenship and an active DoD Secret clearance to perform this work. Advanced degrees include specialized education (Ed.S.) and doctoral degrees (Ph.D. or Psy.D.). These programs include coursework in education and psychology because their work addresses both education and mental health components of students' development.

Patent Attorney and Patent Agent

Roles and responsibilities: A patent attorney is an attorney or agent who is responsible for establishing intellectual property protections and its internationalization for people in society who discover inventions and innovations. Intellectual property includes patents, trademarks, copyrights, trade secrets, and licensing agreements. Patent Agents are professionals from various academic fields who have not passed the state law bar, cannot legal advice nor represent clients. Patent attorneys and patent agents work for clients before the United States Patent and Trademark Office (USPTO) located in Alexandria, Virginia, just outside the Washington, D.C. metro area.

Roles and responsibilities for these legal professionals include decision making to appeal a case to a court, litigating lawsuits for infringement, for a client's issued intellectual property, and conversely, infringing the claims of other clients issued intellectual property. Patent attorneys and patent agents collaborate with other business and engineering experts, computer analysts, manufacturing representatives, and governments that support innovation and invention.

Patent Attorneys and Patent Agents use:

Computers, advanced computer software, national and international search databases, project benchmarking, and sophisticated analytical software tools to do trend analysis and create statistical processes.

Required Skills/Experience: The United States Patent and Trademark Office (USPTO) offers legal services to clients regarding licensing of the invention. Patent attorneys and patent agents may also provide patentability opinions. These professionals have specialized qualifications to represent clients acting in all matters relating to the litigation of patent and trademark law. To file and prosecute intellectual property rights on behalf of their clients' invention, patent attorneys and agents need an adequate background and understanding of sciences, technologies, mathematics, engineering, among other social, health, and psychological discipline areas.

Education Requirements: To be a patent attorney, undergraduate students obtain a bachelor's degree, students begin their undergraduate studies in pre-law courses, engineering, life, and social sciences, and statistics followed by three to four years of law school. Management opportunities for IP professionals representing clients with and without law backgrounds earn either a Ph.D. or a Juris Doctor (J.D.), a professional doctorate in business administration, and management.

Pre-law courses include litigation methods, IP processing, IP assets, business commercialization, valuation, and IP strategies. Some certifications granted by the United States Patent and Trademark Office complement graduate law coursework, such as it is the Global Intellectual Property Academy (GIPA) certification. Research, writing, and communications courses complement the law and engineering curricula. Patent Attorneys also have backgrounds in military services as chief officers, usually from all branches, including the U.S. Coast Guard, U.S. Army, U.S. Air Force, and the U.S. Marines. Some positions in government require U.S. Citizenship and an active DoD Secret clearance to perform this work.

4

CONCLUSION: MARKET YOUR SKILLS

The success of any organization, whether significant multinational or small entrepreneur depends on developing human knowledge and putting that knowledge into practice to improve the business. An organization can be a young group of graduate electrical engineering students, a promising team of nurses discovering enormous patient care innovations, a military platoon creating eyes-on strategic combat processes. In any organization, confidentiality policies protect products or service knowledge. According to policies in strategic partnerships, knowledge is developed over time by the loyalty and intellectual abilities of its employees. The subject matter practices and improvements give the organization a competitive advantage.

In 2014, researchers Ernst and Fischer et al. published the idea of constructing a method for managing intellectual property in collaboration with the processes of research and development. The findings resulted in new knowledge that the outcome of this relationship increases opportunities to influence effective performance. The individual processes and the work performed in each discipline area, such as designing the products' customer requirements, present fundamental cross-functional barriers, or interdependencies. These cross-functional factors are inherent to the steps involved in developing the product.

Awareness of these methods and techniques performed by concept scientists and design engineers helps professionals integrate the cross-functional benefits into the overall manufacturing process. These principles help improve strategic coherence and build competitive advantages. For their customers, these product developers knew that their skills and abilities were critical to proficiently producing quality requirements. It becomes your capital that matters under challenging times. Be mindful of monitoring the time it takes to develop the steps to take, take steps to make your career development valuable. In business, information cultivated by the employee's skills and expertise developed over time is also known as intellectual property or trade secrets.

These valuable secrets and intellectual capital are assets transferred through the continued process of creating and contributing this knowledge. Although organizations work hard to cultivate this complex information, little seems known about how these assets are vital by their employees. Ordinary people need to understand that their inherent talent for creating vocational value over time evolves into career advantages. Organizational strategy theory means that the risk of not being able to transfer knowledge that creates added value strategically is more significant if the employee or small business owner has not integrated a robust risk framework to manage those intangible competencies.

A large part of how you navigate and grow your career will determine how successful the organization is that you represent, whether that company is your own business or a business that you contribute. The level and style of strategy by the vocational choices you make predicates the long-term survival of how much value this creates. You, as a job candidate, should also have the perspective that innovating those strategies should be a long-term priority for success. Simply put, iterative self-invention and your innovative effort for competitiveness among other qualified candidates or you as the business owner should be defined by the continuous practical ideas that you communicate through your skillset and resources.

Some tangible examples of this intellectual capital that you, the employee, can become aware of and how the value of your knowledge has contributed to the firm's overall success:

- Innovation by scientific and engineering discoveries, product or service designs
- Initiatives or publications developed, planned or proposed that helped sell products or services
- The methods of practice, internal policies, techniques, and processes are taken to create products or services
- Company slogans, logos, unique product names or markings
- Customer non-disclosures and agreements
- Strategies developed for business endeavors and marketing planning
- Technologies in the form of systems and software

Publishing Graduate Research Work

Potentially, there are opportunities that a non-scholarly publishing option could be on the horizon for someone telling their life story or graduate students who have published research on a specific topic. In business and industry, change is inevitable. Ever notice how, in recent times, society is dictating that our economy is more service industry-driven than it is product industry-driven? In theory, the products that we purchase are improving, and the services that come with some products seem to expand. The economy and uncertainty wait for no person impacted by the negative shift of being out of work and the ability to earn income. Just as companies monitor the value of how their competitive advantages are performing, employees should do the same to understand their interdependence in their skills and abilities.

One question, and maybe the first question you can ask yourself about producing a device, a theory, or process that you created in academics, is, what do I publish? Look at the subject matter, rationale, and topic significance of what you own in your writings. There is more knowledge about what you prepared than you realize. If you performed any level of research, you analyzed theories, performed data mining, reviewed statistical data, literary references, essays, and articles from databases within your subject matter area. You probably completed a case study project where you formed questions to ask participants that hold experiential knowledge related to your subject matter. Thinking about a subject to write on, you also have gained experiences based on your profession. The framework of your story relies on the events of your life and the activities that occurred.

Publishing a literary idea is another tool that adds value to your career outlook. Building upon the work you started with the study you performed creates a novelty you may not have realized at the time. Filling a gap was the goal and lesson when investigating the answers to the research questions, so this same concept is related to new content development for thinking about topics for publishing. This point may be easier to grasp with collective written thoughts of your life over time. It is the drive of the effort, the creativity of the employee, and meeting the customers' needs that enable companies to be competitive.

Thinking about how to come up with ideas on being competitive often can seem burdensome. Writing ideas coming from research or life events puts you in the unique position of becoming an expert in a field that you have passion. Developing a written project idea improves building and launching a good author brand. Your personal story and statistical facts may be the influence to reach and impact some person or institution from afar and could leverage their economic and social situations.

This unique position is one that you spent many years proving in your professional work to finally leverage the marketing advantages you have to the world as your audience. If change is inevitable in business and industry, then maybe being competitive will matter more if there is a better way to utilize the strategies that you currently use. In graduate business school, I learned from the entrepreneurial and innovation expert Peter F. Drucker that managers in organizations should think about how to fit the product offered by that organization to the process of introducing it to the market. Instead of thinking about how to solve the daily problems, build your strategic thinking towards your strengths and opportunities. In a job interview, every candidate wants to feel like their skills and abilities measure up the tasks listed in the job posting.

Early on in 2000, strategy educators and business consultants Bean & Radford noted that in a transition industrial economy, opportunities to innovate occur in:

- Caring for others with educational opportunities
- Social gatherings where the actions of some influence the actions of others
- Technological, social settings like LinkedIn

- Novel products or services that influence social change

The value of your skills and capabilities as transferred knowledge establishes a sort of "self-organization of products or services." These unique intellectual assets improve your career profile and can lead to new perspectives and interpretations is by:
- Using social technologies to create an intellectual synthesis
- Creating your unique interdisciplinarity
- Adapting interdisciplinarity to enhance your specific set of skills

Entrepreneurship

Innovation is a process as well as it is a possibility. Another possibility that change has several steps. The first step is that the contribution of using the skill and ability of a person to disrupt the economy by conceptualizing a unique idea or make a small improvement on an existing one. The next step is to provide technology transfer or the translation of the concept into a tangible product or service. A next step would be to revisit the business purpose for creating the product or service idea to plan the next steps of supporting the development steps.

The answer to this question provides the reasons for advancing the competitive business positioning. As stated in an earlier chapter, innovation finds a way to promote performing an existing or previous task for the benefit of improving the business purpose, economically, socially, or culturally. Again, the effort and expense that a person invests in his or her career must matter in a way that meets the strategic intent of that person's occupational goals in the long run. You are the entrepreneur of your personal career development and management. This venture is your business.

Entrepreneurs take risks to start the process of innovation. This person is a risk-taker, bearing all the physical and emotional dangers of managing, promoting, and growing a business. An entrepreneur in current times does not engage in the growth of the market after innovation discovery. An argument could exist that the idea of the responsibility of entrepreneurs growing the business. The factor of risk as a responsibility of entrepreneurs originated in the 17th century. Case Western Reserve University Professor Robert D. Hisrich and his research team posited that when taking on a fixed contract with the government, a Frenchman named John Law inadvertently accepted the profits or losses that came along with the deal.

Earlier, we also visited the idea that acquiring an interdisciplinary strategy toward career exploration means disrupting the job market, and growing our skills, improving our vocational advantages. Applying interdisciplinary skills allows us to perform cross-functionally in a competitive career environment. It is notable throughout business literature that when venturing into business, an entrepreneur will need to finance the initial investment for establishing the innovation. In early societies, there were times that the initial effort thought to provide the required finance for developing the invention suffered due to negative risk investment.

Early inventors found out that their innovations once produced used much more capital finance than predicted. Projects or designs once developed, consumed large amounts of capital to launch due to the nature of its improvement. Innovation is a complex process that involves iterative growth steps. Entrepreneurs once were thought to be inventors with only the responsibility to disrupt the economy by conceptualizing a unique idea. Society slowly discovered and accepted the premise that the new definition of the function of innovation becomes integral to the vision of entrepreneurship.

Over time innovation has become a modern enterprise taken on by many entrepreneurs in our history. This skillset gives us another advantage of how to pass on an entrepreneurial performance to others who can learn to do the same. The rationale of the book, coupled with the practical principles of the DISC process, should provide those seeking the same set of goals the facts about how to develop their interdisciplinary skills competitively. Innovation knows no economic boundaries, just as recession, downturns, uncertainty, and inflation.

I believe that with every complicated venture comes some level of maturity and growth. My belief in this concept compares to completing a college degree or completing basic military training. Entrepreneurship has become complicated by three behaviors: the effective use of resources adding value to the innovation, the accomplishment to escape the authority of other people, and the benefit of competitive advantages. A large part of how you navigate and grow your career will determine how successful the organization is that you represent, whether that company is your own business or a business that you contribute. The level and style of strategy by the vocational choices you make predicates the long-term survival of how much value this creates.

Entrepreneurial Creativity and Organization

Ideas to startup a business venture by adding something new in terms of innovation comes from many sources once thought is provoked by the need for independence and motivational will. Paying attention to products or services that already have some consumer applicability, and how these could be improved is a good start. Most new product development lifecycles depend on how consumers use products and apply the services for use and sustainment. Market research and analysis literature can be researched within the library archives in colleges and universities, as well as by marketing professionals looking for opportunities to expand their entrepreneurial vision.

Entrepreneurs occupy various professional careers in our society, including full-time college and university students. Like inventors, entrepreneurs can think of ideas that influence small improvements in current products or services and take on the journey of development and business ownership. Entrepreneurs represent welders, engineers, medical professionals, ex-military, and graduate business students. These individuals desire the feeling of achievement, and to want independence from the stresses of authority. For example, the U.S. military now has credentials and certification programs that enhance cross-functional skills and enable entrepreneurship by awarding licenses to transitioning members such as for single-engine pilots, professional athletic trainers, and physical security careers. People feel that the value of having economic choices, turning those choices into tangible outcomes heightens their motivations to pursue economic, or financial independence.

Creating a novel product or service may be the easiest, less complicated part of the process of innovation. Other factors needed to further inventive ideas into developments that are more complex and challenging in terms of development to growth and sustainment. Managing the process of manufacturing designs may be the most challenging for those people who have not built their project management skills. These factors include understanding finance, new product development methods, the manufacturing process, and marketing the idea to commercialization.

Having a support system from people who specialize or have knowledge of these skillsets provides the added resources entrepreneurs need for success. Plans for an innovative start-up opportunity also come from industry analysis of various products and services. Industry analysis includes investigating the marketing strategies of various companies within different industries, understanding the different product or service benefits, their competitive strengths and weaknesses, pricing structures, and distribution channels. The results of the information collected can summarize competitor analysis techniques. The constant use and re-evaluation of the product's intent from a consumer's perspective help to fuel small improvements over time.

Many opportunities exist for future entrepreneurs working close to the research and development environment; they get the benefit of understanding that there may have been various intentions of the product or service from the start. Understanding how the government played a role in starting some of the greatest inventions thought of by entrepreneurs and inventors is a great resource for research. Inventors are granted intellectual property rights annually by the governments of most industrialized countries that have their registration awarding agencies collocated to major industry hubs around the world. Examples of some of these agencies are the World Trade Organization, the World Intellectual Property Organization, the

U.S. Patent and Trade Offices located worldwide, and the Department of Commerce agencies worldwide.

Databases are easily accessible on the internet and store millions of intellectual property registrations awarded to those inventors living in those countries such as patents, trademarks, and copyrights. You, as a job candidate, should also have the perspective that innovation strategies provide long-term priority for success. Entrepreneurship lends its roots to independence. The simple frustration of having a way of becoming more independent in your career goals drives the motivation of most who venture into invention and innovation.

Having capital and resources to start thinking about developing and processing designs can feel overwhelming, depending on your personal goals for your creative change. The costs associated with this process depend on three things: meeting your capital requirements, adaptability and control of the management decisions, and the responsibilities of profits and losses. The opportunity of career advantages through entrepreneurship helps to provide the inspiration that interdependence gives us.

Simply put, iterative self-invention and your innovative effort for competitiveness among other qualified candidates or you as the business owner should be defined by the continuous practical ideas that you communicate through your skillset and resources. The practices and principles of entrepreneurship involve the coordination of the knowledge of effectively integrating risk, finance, resources, and marketing toward personal goals and vision. By their activities, the coordination of experiences of product teams effectively integrates an organization's corporate mission or vision. The active transference of knowledge between team members helped develop an entrepreneurial attitude toward business tasks. In business, the interdependence between project and program employees and their productivity outcomes drives the goal of attaining a competitive advantage.

The interdependence relationship also speaks to the relevance that, in the end, the best practices of employing the link in skills and abilities reflect the choices, values, the physical and mental needs of the customer. Sharing knowledge, developing business strategies for competitiveness, and making the important decisions necessary for those advantages drive learning and the need for skills development. Interdependent factors illustrated here that provide synergy between knowledge sharing, strategy, and decision making to be competitive revealed new ideas for influencing the skills and priorities that strengthen career development.

- Personal performance assessment
- Leadership
- Competence
- Market positioning
- Team oriented
- Change management
- Education and training

Constructivism is the theory that suggests that people create their ability to learn. It establishes the idea that people learn through their own experiences and understanding. This theory of constructivism supports the knowledge that people acknowledge the world through the reflection of those experiences. Students comprehend new wisdom from what was previously learned and understood. This new knowledge is integrated, processed, and efficiently utilized to create unique outcomes. Interdisciplinarity requires students and professionals to be inquisitive, ask questions, invoke exploration, and make assessments. Acquiring interdisciplinary skills provides students the benefit of making connections between complex concepts that differ in theory and application. Some of these benefits to consider:

- Motivation is a major factor influencing students when topics that fit their interests. Life experiences, coupled with learning, tend to change and help connect these choices.
- Various perspectives from topics of interest help strengthen the influences that drive students' motivation.
- Inherent to the choice of topics of interest to the student is critical thinking skills.
- Looking across the disciplinary boundaries of varied subject areas helps to develop the student's skill of comparing and contrasting.
- Various perspectives from topics of interest also help strengthen the student's ability to synthesize ideas and formulate alternatives regarding new knowledge.
- As students gain coherence to varied topics coupling these with their life's experiences helps to strengthen their critical thinking and to learn about research methodologies
- Creativity cultivates a student's learning ability to comprehend more about interdisciplinarity and its application.
- Students should remain open-minded about the innovations of higher learning and traditional disciplines.

Education innovation keeps us focused on our mission to begin to invent our own goals to accomplish career advantages. Continuous learning is necessary to stay relevant in the job market, whether in industry or to consult independently. These experiences ensure awareness and ensure your abilities to learn how to perform technical and social tasks. Throughout these chapters, one perspective has been on the importance of being dependent on your competencies. The other aspect was to decide on a competitive framework necessary to understand how to translate them into specific knowledge capital. In the end, we begin to understand the definition, purpose, and how to apply these perspectives and understand the concept of entrepreneurship. Innovation comes from the transference of knowledge by entrepreneurs who understand the product, the vision of its purpose, the method of manufacturing it, and commercializing it for the benefit of introducing economic or technological change.

Who gets the benefit from the knowledge in this book will get a practical, experiential understanding of how it applies to their confidence and career strategies? Postgraduate researchers and undergraduate business school students and cohorts, those who are studying physical and social sciences, information technology, healthcare, economics, policy, engineering development, and innovation. Students may get good ideas to further write about their efforts in moving knowledge forward, covering current research trends and gaps. Business and technology leaders and managers researching policies, protocols, and best practices in product development can absorb the text to expand their human intellectual capital in an exploration of small improvements.

Acknowledgments

To both my brave parents who survived insurmountable challenges throughout their lives. My strength, tenacity and will to live comes from My mother. My father, who survived the trials of Vietnam, and he gave me duty, respect, and the skills of survival. They both gave me the skills to understand the concepts of competitive advantage. To my family, my grandmother, my Native American heritage. My business partner and my life partner Theresa Kearse has helped me position myself to entrepreneurship more clearly. I want to show my appreciation to the U.S. Army for enhancing my electronic technology background, providing me with specialized technical training and life experiences that have improved my mental courage, discipline, and endurance.

I completed my case study dissertation and began writing. I was excited to get my message of career interdependency and interdisciplinarity to those interested. This book is the fruit born out of the research work that I formulated from the lessons at Capella University, the University of the District of Columbia, the several of the black women-owned law firms in Washington, D.C.

Capella University provided me with the opportunity no other school would. The schools' online and in-person sessions gave me the exposure of integrating critical thinking with students from Asia, Africa, Europe, South America, and India. The practice-based scholarly training challenged me academically, but against all the odds, I received both the Master of Business Administration and the Doctorate in Business Administration.

About the Author

Walter K. Davis, DBA, MBA, is a practicing engineering liaison, publishing author, and doctoral business school student mentor. For the past twenty years, he has provided engineering and technology consultancy to Fortune 500 companies and federal government agencies. Walter has provided support for new product development to research & development strategy, manufacturing process capability, and intellectual property guidance to transitioning entrepreneurs. He is a U.S. Army veteran, where he supported special operations in signals intelligence and system integration. He has worked to integrate innovation in intellectual property management, manufacturing process capability, and electronic sensor systems for automotive, aerospace, biomedical, and consumer appliance applications domestically and internationally.

Walter graduated Magna Cum Laude from Capella University, earning an MBA, with a focus in Operations/Project Management and a Doctorate of Business Administration, with a research emphasis in Strategy and Innovation. He earned a graduate certificate in Project Management from the University of California, Irvine, received a Bachelor's degree in Electronic Technology and received specialized training in Intellectual Property Law. Walter plans to develop a blog and give practical, experiential support to his young daughter Audrey in STEM education and the social sciences.

Consult with Walter, let us discuss

- Providing seminar and workshop experiences in Career Advantages: An Interdisciplinary Approach
- Allow me to guide on applying the DISC model in your career strategy for college and university students, transitioning military veterans, future entrepreneurs, and innovators.
- Postgraduate and graduate students mentoring
- Specialized guidance for innovators considering applying for Non-provisional and provisional Hardware Patents, Trademarks, and Copyrights.

🌐 Find, Share, and learn more about the content in the book, do not hesitate to ask questions and have them answered on social media.

@ www.LinkedIn.com/in/WalterKDavis2020

✉ Send Email: wdavis24@capellauniversity.edu

References

Bean, R., and Radford, R. (2000). Powerful Products: Strategic Management of Successful New Product Development. New York: AMACOM. Retrieved from https://www.worldcat.org/title/powerful-products-strategic-management-of-successful-new-product-development/oclc/43445716.

Battagello, F. M., Cricelli, L., & Grimaldi, M. (2016). Benchmarking strategic resources and business performance via an open framework. International Journal of Productivity and Performance Management, 65(3), 324-350. DOI:10.1108/IJPPM-08-2014-0129.

Demartini, P., and Paoloni, P. (2013). Implementing an Intellectual Capital Framework in Practice. Journal of Intellectual Capital, 14(1).

Douglas, F. (from 1817-1882). The life and times of Frederick Douglass: In Autobiographies (New York: Library of America, 1994), 527. Retrieved from https://amazon.com/Life-Times-Frederick-Douglass-Words/dp/B001R9EKX6.

Drucker, P.F. (1985). Innovation and Entrepreneurship: Practice and Principles (New York: Harper and Row), p. 138.

Ernst, H., and Fischer, M. (2014). Integrating the R&D and patent functions: Implications for new product performance. 31(S1), 118–132. DOI: 10.1111/jpim.12196.

Grant, R. M. (2010). Contemporary Strategy Analysis (7th ed., combined text and case version). West Sussex, UK: John Wiley & Sons.

Gallo, J. L. (2017). The effect of an interdisciplinary career exploration course on college students' career decision-making and career decision-making self-efficacy. ProQuest Dissertations & Theses Global. Available from https://link.springer.com/article/10.1007%2Fs41686-019-00032-3 (1985964021).

Greco, M., Cricelli L., & Grimaldi, M. (2013). A strategic management framework of tangible and intangible assets. European Management Journal, 31(1). DOI: 10.1016/j.emj.2012.10.005.

Hisrich, R.D., Peters, M.P., and Shephard, D. (2005). Entrepreneurship (6th ed., combined text and case version). New York, NY: McGraw-Hill.

Jaffe, E. (2009). Crossing boundaries: The growing enterprise of interdisciplinary research. APS Observer, 22(5), 10–13.

Jones, C. (2009). "Interdisciplinary Approach - Advantages, Disadvantages, and the Future Benefits of Interdisciplinary Studies," ESSAI: Vol. 7, Article 26. Available at: http://dc.cod.edu/essai/vol7/iss1/26.

NCDA, National Career Development Association (2008). Retrieved from http://lifeworkps.com/HPH/NCDA/NCDA-Policy-Statement-on-Seven-Stages-of-CD.html.

Occupational Safety and Health Administration U.S. Department of Labor, OSHA 3328-05R (2009). Pandemic Influenza Preparedness and Response Guidance for Healthcare Workers and Healthcare Employers. Retrieved from https://www.osha.gov/Publications/OSHA_pandemic_health.pdf

Perez-Cano, C., and Villan-Altamirano, J. (2013). Factors that influence the propensity to patent. Engineering Management Journal, 25(3), 355-374. http://DOI/abs/10.1080/10429247.2013.11431980.

Salvetat, D., Géraudel, M., and D'armagnac, S. (2013). Inter-organizational knowledge management in a coopetitive context in the aeronautics and space industry. Knowledge Management Research & Practice, 11(3), 265-277. https://doi.org/10.1057/kmrp.2012.6.

Shoemaker, P. J. H., Krupp, S., & Howland, S. (2013). Strategic Leadership: The Essential Skills. Harvard Business Review, 1-5.

Shell, E. R. (2018). The Job: Work and Its Future in a Time of Radical Change. New York, NY: Currency: Penguin Random House https://www.amazon.com/Job-Work-Future-Radical-Change/dp/0451497252.

Spender, J. C. (2015). Business Strategy: Managing Uncertainty, Opportunity, and Enterprise. New York, NY: Oxford University Press.

Sinha, C. (2016). Rethinking interdisciplinarity in social sciences: Is it a new revolution or paradox? 44-66. https://uca.edu/mat/facultystaff/jeff-whittingham/

Super, D. E., Savickas, M. L., and Super, C. M. (1996). "The Life-span, Life-space Approach to Careers." Pp. 121-178 in Career Choice and Development. 3d ed., edited by D. Brown, L. Brooks, and Associates. San Francisco, CA: Jossey-Bass.

Survilaite, S., Tamosiuniene, R., & Shatrevich, V. (2015). Intellectual capital approach to modern management through the perspective of a company's value-added. Business: Theory & Practice, 16(1), 31-44. DOI:10.3846/btp.2015.553.

Teece, D. J. (2014). The Foundations of Enterprise Performance: Dynamic and Ordinary Capabilities in an (Economic) Theory of Firms. Academy of Management Perspectives, 28(4), 328-352.

Thompson, A., Peteraf, M., Gamble, J., & Strickland, A. J. III. (2012). Crafting & executing strategy: The quest for competitive advantage: Concepts and cases. (18th ed.). McGraw-Hill/Irwin.

Takeuchi, H., & Nonaka, I. (1986). The new product development game. Harvard Business Review, 64(1), 137-146. http://www.agilepractice.eu/wp-content/uploads/2016/09/Product-Development-Scrum-1986.pdf.

Terziovski, M. (2010). Innovation practice and its performance implications in small and medium enterprises (SMEs) in the manufacturing sector: a resource-based view. Strategic Management Journal, 31(8), 892-902. DOI: 10.1002/smj.841.

United States Government Accountability Office (2013). Report to congressional committees. Intellectual property: Assessing factors that affect patent infringement litigation could help improve patent quality. GOA-13-465. 1-24.

Ulrich, T. K., and Eppinger, D. S. (2016). Product Design and Development. (5th ed.). New York, NY: McGraw-Hill.

United States Patent and Trademark Office (2016). 2014-2018 Strategic Plan. 1-38. www.uspto.gov/strategicptlan.

Yaseen, S. G., Dajani, D., & Hasan, Y. (2016). The Impact of Intellectual Capital on the Competitive Advantage: Applied Study in Jordanian Telecommunication Companies. Computers in Human Behavior, 62, 168-175. Retrieved from https://www.sciencedirect.com/science/article/pii/S0747563216 302473.